Chancel Screens Since the Reformation

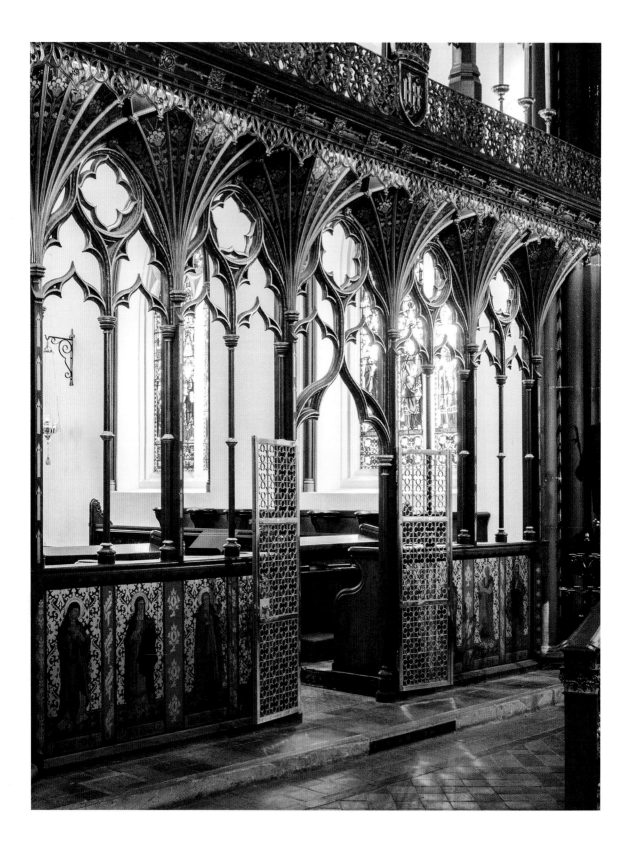

CHANCEL SCREENS
SINCE THE REFORMATION

Edited by Mark Kirby

Proceedings of the
Ecclesiological Society Conference,
London, 2019

ISBN: 978-0-946823-26-0
ISSN: 1460-4213

Published 2020 by the Ecclesiological Society
c/o The Society of Antiquaries of London
Burlington House
Piccadilly
London
W1V 0HS

The Ecclesiological Society is a registered charity. Charity no. 210501.
Join the society at: www.ecclsoc.org

The views expressed in this publication are those of the authors and do not necessarily represent those of the Ecclesiological Society or its officers.

Designed by Vera Fabiankova
Printed in the UK by Henry Ling Ltd, at the Dorset Press, Dorchester, DT1 1HD

Cover image: The chancel screen at St John's, Leeds, c.1630–34. (Photo: Graham White)

Frontispiece: The screen at St Paul's, Brighton by R. C. Carpenter (1846–48), successively remodelled by G. F. Bodley in 1870 and later. (Photo: John Roberts, 2018)

CHANCEL SCREENS
SINCE THE REFORMATION

Contributors

THE REVD DR PETER DOLL is Canon Librarian of Norwich Cathedral, and is the author of several books addressing the relationship between theology, liturgy and church architecture.

DR LUCY WRAPSON is a senior paintings conservator at the Hamilton Kerr Institute, University of Cambridge, specialising in the conservation and technical study of polychrome medieval wood and panel paintings.

TREVOR COOPER is a Vice-President of the Ecclesiological Society. He has had a life-long interest in churches, his research particularly focusing on church interiors of the first half of the seventeenth century and the future of church buildings.

DR MARK KIRBY is Chairman of Council of the Ecclesiological Society, and is a Research Fellow in architectural history at Lincoln College, University of Oxford. He is currently writing a monograph on the College's Chapel (built 1629–31).

JOHN ROBERTS read History and Fine Arts at Cambridge, and after a career in publishing has returned to study, for a DPhil in architectural history at the University of Oxford. His subject is roodscreens in the nineteenth century.

ANDREW DERRICK is Deputy Chairman of Council of the Ecclesiological Society and a Director of the Architectural History Practice (AHP). AHP have led on Taking Stock, an architectural and historical review of Catholic Churches in England and Wales (https://taking-stock.org.uk/).

CLARE PRICE is Head of Casework at the Twentieth Century Society, and is researching the design of the Anglican church between the wars for a DPhil at the University of Oxford.

Preface

This volume – *Chancel Screens Since the Reformation* – contains the proceedings of the 2019 Ecclesiological Society Conference. It is, in some respects, a history of ambivalence. The pre-Reformation rood screen served a clearly understood function. Its component features of dado, open screen, rood loft and Rood variously provided features for decoration and the deployment of iconography, culminating in the Rood itself – the predominant image in most church interiors. And the screen's very nature as a point of division between the people's space of the nave and the priests' space of the chancel went broadly without challenge.

The Reformation changed all that. The painted figures of angels, prophets, kings and saints on the dado were literally defaced, their presence no longer necessary to evoke or intermediate prayer – indeed they became superstitious obstacles to prayer. As the most prominent and most devotionally significant image in the church, the Rood – the figure of the crucified Christ, usually with Mary and John either side – likewise had to go. With the Rood gone and the burning of candles frowned upon, the rood loft had to be removed too, not so much because it was in itself liturgically offensive to Reformed sensibilities but because it no longer served a purpose and might be a dangerous reminder of what had been lost, or a facilitator of its return.

The essays here address how subsequent generations thought about chancel screens once their original purposes had been removed or declared unacceptable. The book starts with two chapters of critical context. Peter Doll has kindly supplemented the papers given by the speakers at the conference, and describes the theological origins and evolution of the notion of a barrier or divide in Judeo-Christian places of worship – from Moses' Tabernacle in the Wilderness up to today. Themes from here about sacred space (or not), liminality, and evolving doctrinal attitudes towards Communion then echo in each of the chapters which follow. Lucy Wrapson sets out the nature of the rood screen as it stood on the eve of the Reformation. Importantly, here we see what it was that the Reformation rejected, posing the question as to what screens were there for from that point onwards.

And here is where the ambivalence begins. There never has been a single Church of England understanding of what a chancel screen is, or even what it is called (as the consciously varying terminology in this volume demonstrates). Common threads of understanding connect the generations around the themes of eucharistic space – understood with differing notions of sanctity about the space itself – and the practical out-workings of eucharistic liturgy. Other than in the period following a Royal Order of Elizabeth I in 1561 mandating that there be a chancel screen in parish churches, nearly every subsequent generation has shown some degree of equivocation on the subject.

From the distance of half a millennium it might seem strange that chancel screens should have survived the Reformation at all. But survive they did, and, as Trevor Cooper demonstrates, they did more than just survive. Some of the new chancel screens erected in the early seventeenth century are significant and expensive examples of fine craftsmanship. Those which are not nevertheless testify to an abiding conviction that churches needed to have screens. Even the Parliamentary iconoclasts of the 1640s only targeted screens with unacceptable quantities of statuary and imagery on them rather than removing them as an entire genre.

Nevertheless the instinct that churches needed to have screens was clearly in decline. When the Great Fire of London destroyed 82 parish churches, only two of those rebuilt were fitted with a chancel screen. As I describe in my own chapter, these two were justified by their enthusiastic rectors by reference to the practice of the Early Church and were as much about making statements of Anglican identity as they were about declaring eucharistic doctrine. Other church builders did not feel the same need, and the Long Eighteenth Century is entirely missing from this book for the obvious reason that it was a predominantly screenless period during which no meaningful purpose could be found for the notion of chancels or chancel screens in the auditory church. The few that do exist are mostly whimsically "Gothick" rather than driven by any particular liturgical need.

John Roberts and Andrew Derrick take us through the nineteenth century and it is striking to see how many of the same arguments about screens were made both in the Church of England and in the Roman Catholic Church – the latter after the Second Catholic Relief Act of 1791 permitted Roman Catholic churches to be built. These arguments addressed much the same questions about ecclesial identity that were raised in the seventeenth century about what the Church was, whose inheritance formed the nature of the Church then, and what its liturgical priorities needed to be. Attitudes to chancel screens became emblematic of how you answered these questions. Not only were many of the arguments the same but sometimes the same people made them, and the name of Pugin is prominent in both chapters. The emotional intensity of debate at times matched that of the Reformation period itself and it remains curious that this period saw both the revival in setting up new rood screens in both existing and newly-built churches and, at the same time, the removal of very many surviving medieval screens.

It might again be reasonably asked why, in the twentieth century, chancel screens continued to be erected in new parish churches if, indeed, attitudes across the spectrum of Churchmanship had become so equivocal. Clare Price shows how Percy Dearmer and the Alcuin Club maintained the flame, and provided an intellectual and ecclesiological foundation that could be built upon when the end of the First World War cried out for new ways to memorialise the fallen. Chancel screens – once the subject of deliberation by kings and prelates – now found themselves debated by Diocesan Advisory Committees.

But at least there is something still to debate. Attendees at the conference heard how screens still appear on DAC agendas for adaptation, re-ordering or re-locating to a different church. And at St George's, Ivychurch (Kent) plans are ongoing for the creation of a new twenty-first century chancel screen, responding to a sense that there needed to be a separation of space between the worship area of the chancel and the increasingly community-based use of the nave. We look forward to hearing how these plans progress.

Most of what is in this book represents new scholarship. Collectively, the contributors have highlighted the centrality of the role played by chancel screens since the Reformation, and how they are a bellwether for broader theological and ecclesiological shifts in thinking. We hope that this will stimulate further thinking and research.

At the practical level, the authors and our design team have also worked on these chapters against the backdrop of 2020, an *annus horibilis* if ever there was one. I am therefore doubly grateful to them for bringing this volume to completion.

Mark Kirby
Chairman of Council
The Ecclesiological Society

chair@ecclsoc.org

Chapter 1

Dividing it Unites, Concealing it Reveals: A Theology of the Chancel Screen

PETER M. DOLL

'We have now to contend for the great principles of Catholic antiquity … It is not a struggle for taste or ornament, but a contention for vital principles.'

Augustus Welby Pugin, *A Treatise on Chancel Screens and Rood Lofts*[1]

For Pugin, the presence of a chancel screen was not an ornamental option, but a vital principle of church design. While in Orthodox churches this remains the case, it was a battle Pugin lost within his own Roman Catholic community, and which has even failed to protect from destruction a great number of historic screens in English churches. What, then, is the vital principle to which Pugin alludes?

The essays in this volume discuss how the generations after the Reformation each in turn sought to address that same question. But they were not starting anew, and to understand the origins of the chancel screen and its theological significance we must look back far beyond the Christian Church proper to the worship of the Israelite people in the Tent of Meeting or Tabernacle, the Temple in Jerusalem and the theology of Creation they embodied. The Tabernacle and the Temple were built to be a microcosm of the seven days of Creation and thus to embody the whole relationship between the Creation and God, time and eternity, immanence and transcendence. In these structures the Veil of the Temple was the meeting place between time and eternity. The Christian church building is the lineal descendant of the Temple and the chancel screen of the Veil.

The story of God's people as interpreted through both the Old and New Testaments is a repeated pattern of God's creation, humanity's sinful rebellion against God's providential order, and then God's repeated re-creation. The Temple and the church building and their worship encompass the sweep of this salvation history and its pattern of creation, rebellion, divine forgiveness, and pointing to eschatological fulfilment. The Veil and the screen stand symbolically and functionally at the interface between Earth and Heaven, humanity and God. These boundaries mark what is often called 'liminal space', defined by physical and spiritual thresholds.[2]

The sacrificial rites of the Temple and the Church's eucharistic liturgy (which, depending on one's theology, is either a participation in or commemoration of Christ's sacrifice on the Cross) operate at and through this juncture of Earth and Heaven. In the church it has taken the characteristic form of a barrier or screen. Over the centuries this structure has appeared in a wide variety of forms and been given various names, from the *cancelli* in the early basilicas to the templon screen, *iconostasis*, chancel screen, rood screen, *pulpitum*, *jubé*, *tramezzo*, *reja*, *Lettner*, and many others. Like every aspect of church buildings they have been subject to the vagaries of fashion. They have been attacked ostensibly for creating privileged spaces for the clergy, as unaesthetic disruptors of interior vistas, and as barriers to lay participation in the liturgy. In its origins, however, the screen was intended to facilitate rather than prevent the shaping of the believer's relationship with God according to the pattern of Christ, until he or she attains the full stature of humanity in the likeness of Christ.

Articulating and representing the relationship between divine transcendence and earthly immanence is fundamental to the Jewish and Christian tradition.[3] In the Biblical account of Creation, on the second day God creates the firmament that he calls Heaven. His act brings order to the chaos waters by separating them into two places, above and below the firmament (Genesis 1: 6–8). On the third day God gathers the waters under the heavens and makes the dry land appear, thus creating the earth, on which he brings forth plants, creatures, and finally, on the sixth and last day of his work, man as the crown of his creation. God gives to humans, alone of all creation, the capacity to know him and relate to him, but he also sets limits on them, commanding them not to eat of the tree of the knowledge of good and evil (Genesis 2:17). Human obedience is necessary in order for Heaven and Earth to be held together. Before the Fall, all creation is united and without any division.

Adam and Eve, however, presume on their intimacy with God to seek to be like God himself, knowing good and evil, and they eat of the tree. They are expelled from Paradise, and a veil falls between God and man. After the disasters of Babel and the Flood, God chooses Abraham to be the father of many nations. In the Exodus the Lord inaugurates the great deed of deliverance which will bring his people Israel out of slavery in Egypt and into the Promised Land. The climax of Exodus is a new beginning that God offers his people, the restoration of Creation and the rejoining of Heaven and Earth and of God dwelling with his people, in the gift of the Tabernacle. (What applies to the Tabernacle applies equally to the Temple which succeeded it.) The six stages of the construction of the Tent (Exodus 40:17–33) are understood in Jewish Midrash as recapitulating the six days of creation in Genesis 1.[4] In the Tabernacle, the Holy of Holies corresponds to Heaven, the Veil to the material web that conceals the throne of God from human apprehension.

The Tabernacle and the Temple of Jerusalem

The Tabernacle and then the Temple is God's decisive act to remove the separation that had come between him and his people after the Fall. It is a new Creation, a microcosm of both Heaven and Earth there in the midst of God's people. God brought Heaven with himself down to Earth; God chose to dwell invisibly with his people in the Holy of Holies, his Throne being the Mercy-Seat on the Ark of the Covenant containing the tablets of the Ten Commandments. It was an anticipation of the Incarnation which was to follow, God in human flesh in Jesus Christ. Only one person ever entered the Holy of Holies, the High Priest, on one day in the year, Yom Kippur (the Day of Atonement), to sprinkle the Mercy Seat with the blood of sacrifice to cover the sins of the people.

The Veil of the Temple identified the nature of the Holy of Holies at the same time as it separated it from the Holy Place. According to Exodus 26:31, the Veil was of four colours, woven blue, purple, and scarlet thread with fine linen. According to Josephus and Philo (two Jewish commentators of the first century AD) the four colours were emblems of the four elements of which the physical creation was made: red being fire; blue, air; purple, water; and linen, earth.[5] In this way, the stuff of physical creation concealed Heaven and the Glory of God. It was a concealment, however, that also revealed. If the Veil was not there, then neither would Heaven be there. It would simply be undifferentiated space. The Veil united the spaces at the same time it distinguished their functional and symbolic identities.

The architecture of the Temple and the Creation it embodied is inseparable from the Gospel, from the New Testament, the Church, and the church building that all emerged from Judaism in the first century AD. The evangelists understand the saving work of Jesus through the only means known to them, the Hebrew Scriptures. God carries out his great work of redemption as he has always done, through the pattern of Creation. John the Evangelist lets us know in no uncertain terms the shape of the account he has to share: '*In the beginning* was the Word' (John 1:1). At the climax of his unfolding of the mystery of the Incarnation, when he states, 'The Word became flesh and dwelt among us; ... we have beheld his glory' (John 1:14), the literal translation of 'dwelt' is 'tabernacled': Jesus is the living Temple, God among his people whose Glory is concealed by the Veil of his human flesh.

When Jesus comes to the end of his life, his final week is a new week of Creation. Good Friday is the sixth day of the week (recapitulating the original creation of man), and Pontius Pilate presents him to his people saying, 'Behold the man!' (John 19:5). Jesus is the true human being, the true Image of God, and his final statement, 'It is finished' (John 19:30) echoes the completion of Creation in Genesis. John focusses his story again and again on the Temple and on Jesus' self-identification with it: 'Destroy this Temple and in three days I will raise it up' (John 2:19, 21). The new Creation in Jesus is followed by the new Exodus. He is the Passover lamb whose bones are not broken (Exodus 12:46, John 19:33, 37) and whose blood poured out rescues his people from death (Exodus 22:22, John 19:34, cf. 1 John 5:6–8).

The synoptic evangelists link the Incarnation to the Temple Veil (Luke 23:45) torn in two at the death of Jesus and thus opening the way from Earth to Heaven for those who believe in him. Luke then associates the Ascension with the Temple (Luke 24:51–52, Acts 1:9–10), describing his journey to Heaven as the moment the Great High Priest returned to the Holy of Holies; the cloud that took him out of the sight of the disciples was the cloud of incense, the veiling symbol of God's presence.

The rest of the New Testament also repeatedly places Jesus' saving work in the context of the Temple. When St Paul in his Letter to the Romans describes Jesus as 'an expiation by his blood, to be received by faith' (Rom 3:25), the Greek for 'expiation', ἱλαστηριον *hilasterion*, literally means the Mercy-Seat on the Ark of the Covenant in the Holy of Holies. The Letter to the Hebrews includes an extended meditation on Christ as the Great High Priest offering to God the sacrifice of the Cross in the heavenly Temple: 'Since we have confidence to enter the sanctuary by the blood of Jesus, by the new and living way which he opened for us through the curtain, that, through his flesh, and since we have a great high priest over the house of God, let us draw near with a true heart in full assurance of faith, with our hearts sprinkled clean from an evil conscience and our bodies washed with pure water' (Hebrews 20:19–23). The writer addresses his audience of Jewish Christians as a priestly people who follow the Yom Kippur rites previously reserved to the High Priest alone in order to enter the Holy of Holies. The final book of the Bible, the Revelation to John, translates the former ritual of the now destroyed (AD 70) Jerusalem Temple to the heavenly New Jerusalem which is entirely the Temple. Where once only the High Priest bore the Name of God on his forehead (Exodus 28:38), now the whole priestly people does so (Revelation 20:4). As all of Creation returns to its origin in God, there is no longer any reason for a Temple to exist: 'And I saw no temple in the city, for its temple is the Lord God the Almighty and the Lamb' (Revelation 21:22). The theology of Hebrews and Revelation becomes particularly significant for Anglican church building, as they help define eucharistic theology in the seventeenth and eighteenth centuries.

The Fathers and the theological beginnings of Church architecture

The centrality of the Temple to the New Testament reflects a trajectory that drew early Christians away from their fellow Jews, particularly in the wake of the destruction of the Temple building.[6] The Catholic theologian John McDade summarises the divergence in this way:

> The Pharisees, the forerunners of Rabbinic Judaism, proposed the sanctification of Israel by its faithful observance of all the prescriptions of the Torah, thereby embodying the holiness and separation proper to the Temple itself. Christ-centred Jews … drew instead upon the cultic and sacrificial cult of the Temple worship for their interpretation of the death of Christ. … The community came to understand that the events on the Mount of Calvary should be interpreted in the light of the priestly atoning ritual on the Mount of the Temple.[7]

This consciousness of the fulfilment of the Temple tradition in the sacrifice of the Eucharist will come to have a definitive influence on the shape of the Christian church building.

In the early Christian basilicas, the screen began life as the *cancelli*, a kind of crowd control barrier, such as is still to be seen in San Clemente in Rome. It protected the clergy, singers, and other officiants from the press of the crowds of worshippers and kept open the processional routes. Even so, the symbolic is evident alongside the practical. The sanctuary space projecting out into the congregation shows how heaven comes into the midst of earth in Christ. Next an architrave was built on columns on top of the waist-high barrier, as in the eleventh-century cathedral on the Venetian island of Torcello. The chancel screen in the fourth-century St Peter's Basilica in Rome included spiral 'Solomonic' columns said to be *spolia* from the Temple. By the eleventh century in the East, icons were being hung on these screens and they began to take the form of the iconostasis familiar to us today.[8]

In both East and West, the assumption of the continuity between the Temple and the Church was the foundation of the theology both of the Eucharist and of church buildings.[9] As the Orthodox Bishop Basil Osborne has written, 'The connection between the Eucharistic Liturgy and the furnishings of the Jerusalem Temple have been part of the Eastern tradition since at least the beginning of the third century.'[10] Orthodox theology, worship, and building in particular have embraced the tensions inherent in the double character of sacramental religion, the indivisibility of the material and immaterial, the visible and the invisible, the revealed and the concealed, the earthly and the heavenly. As the fifteenth-century liturgical commentator St Symeon of Thessalonike explained:

> The church is double on account of its division into the space of the sanctuary and that which is outside the sanctuary, and it images Christ himself, who is likewise double, being at once God and man, both invisible and visible. And the church likewise images man, who is compounded of (visible) body and (invisible) soul.[11]

The icon screen, like the Veil of the Temple, is the visible threshold of the invisible. Like the Incarnation, it is a division that unites Heaven and Earth. Even as it conceals the sanctuary, it reveals the presence of the invisible Heaven.

Symeon as liturgical theologian had his Western counterpart in the thirteenth-century Bishop Guillaume Durand of Mende. His *Rationale divinorum officiorum*, a liturgical commentary that would later influence the founders of the Cambridge Camden Society, starts from the assumption that 'From both of these, namely, from the tabernacle and the temple, doth our material church take its form.'[12] Through the encounters with Jerusalem of pilgrims and crusaders, both the Biblical Temple and the more recent structures on the Temple Mount exercised a powerful influence on church building in the West. Buildings and sites as various as the Campo Santo at Pisa, the Abbey of St Denis and the Sainte-Chapelle in Paris were conceived as equivalents of the Temple. Crusaders even associated the Dome of the Rock with the renewal of Solomon's Temple. Both it and the Church of the Holy Sepulchre shaped the building of many centrally planned churches throughout

Western Europe, not least the Temple Church in London. Theologians and mystics from St Augustine to St Bede, St Bernard of Clairvaux, St Bonaventure and St Thomas Aquinas construct ecclesiologies based on a Temple typology.[13]

From the Middle Ages to the modern day

For the Western church, the era *par excellence* of the screened church was the Middle Ages. The common accusation is that as the church became increasingly clericalised, so the clergy sought to restrict proximity to the Sacrament, to keep the laity at as great a distance as possible. If the only celebration of the Mass was at the high altar, this accusation might be tenable, but the fact is that Masses were celebrated at altars all around these churches where the laity might participate extremely intimately – one need think only of the famous painting in the National Gallery of the Mass of St Giles of around 1500. Christ was equally present at each Mass. Even with a screen, as Eamon Duffy has pointed out, 'if the laity sometimes passed through the screen to the mystery, the mystery sometimes moved out to meet them'.[14] Other recent studies, notably by Jacqueline E. Jung, have also provided better informed and more nuanced understandings of the way screens were perceived and used in the Middle Ages, putting paid to the myth that they existed in order to separate and exclude. 'Choir screens fulfilled a wide variety of incorporative functions…. They united the discrete spaces of choir and nave while simultaneously asserting the integrity of each spatial unity.'[15]

Rather than marking the eclipse of the ancient Temple associations, the Renaissance and Reformation actually prompted a re-energising of these motifs as Catholics and Protestants vied to claim for themselves the true Biblical inheritance. In building their American empire, the Spanish stipulated the Temple as a model for both church and urban planning.[16] If the Temple remained an important point of reference, screens did not always retain their honoured place. Catholic Reformation churches conceived by the Jesuits, exemplified by the *Gesù* in Rome, built shallow chancels and eschewed screens entirely. In the reformed Church of England, however, despite the prevalence of iconoclasm, the chancel screen maintained an officially mandated presence. The church Orders of Queen Elizabeth of October 1561 specified that chancel screens should be retained and that the communion table should be set altarwise at the east end under the tables of the Decalogue, other than during the celebration of the communion.

In England, theological and architectural interest in the Temple was only part of a widespread 'obsession' with its relation to Jewish history because the English (like other nations) understood their land to be the 'new Israel' and themselves to be a chosen people.[17] Even for the natural philosopher and mathematician Sir Isaac Newton, the form and geometry of the Temple were keys to unlocking the mysteries of God. Anglican theologians – particularly those 'avant-garde conformists' following the example of Queen Elizabeth, Richard Hooker and Lancelot Andrewes – understood English churches and the worship in them in light of the Patristic typological models with which this account began. Hooker argued that Temple and church ought to have the same form and that therefore churches should retain their chancel screens:

> Our churches are places provided that the people might there assemble themselves in due and decent manner, according to their several degrees and order. Which thing being common unto us with Jews, we have in this respect our churches divided by certain partitions … there being in ours … but one partition, the cause whereof at the first (as it seemeth) was, that as many as were capable of the holy mysteries might there assemble themselves….[18]

Here Hooker refers to the Anglican practice of gathering the congregation in the nave for the Liturgy of the Word and then priest and people moving together into the chancel for the Liturgy of the Eucharist. This practice was a fulfilment of the theology of the Letter to the Hebrews and Revelation that Christians by baptism into Christ are a priestly people. Where once only the High Priest would have entered the Holy of Holies behind the Veil, the movement of the faithful through the chancel screen from Earth to Heaven was a profound expression of the priesthood of all believers.[19]

For Hooker, it was only right that Christian churches should imitate the Temple not only in structure but also in 'the majesty and holiness of the place, where God is worshipped'.[20] Those decorative elements which would become standard features in Anglican churches – the tables of the Ten Commandments with the Cherubim, Moses and Aaron, the cloudy glory of the *Shekinah*, and the *Tetragrammaton* of the Holy Name – all located the Church of England's Eucharist in the Holy of Holies in the Temple.

Joseph Mede, the leading Hebrew scholar, affirmed that God's divine presence was in the church just as it was in the Temple. In his sermon *The Reverence of God's House* (1636) he insisted on the continuing significance of the Jewish witness, referring back to St Paul's interpretation of the Temple:

You will say, What is all this to us, now in the time of the Gospell? I answer, Yes. For did not Christ ordaine the holy Eucharist to be the memorial of his Name in the New Testament? … And what if I should affirme, that Christ is as much present here, as the Lord was upon the Mercy-seat between the Cherubins? Why should not then the Place of this Memoriall under the Gospell have some semblable sanctitie to that, where the Name of God was recorded in the Law?

In a word, all those sacred Memorialls of the Jewish Temple are both comprehended and excelled in this One of the Christians, the Sacrifices, Shewbread, and Ark of the Covenant; Christ's Bodie and Bloud in the Eucharist being all these unto us in the New Testament, agreeably to that of the Apostle, [Romans 3:25]. 'God hath set forth Iesus Christ to be our ἱλαστηριον *through faith in his bloud*', that is, our *Propitiatory* or *Mercy seat*.[21]

The unity of his witness with the Scriptures and the early Fathers could not be stronger. Figures 1 and 2 offer a visual summary of an Anglican adherence to this Biblical and Patristic typology of old, new, and heavenly Temples.

This typological understanding of Anglican worship would continue to be a powerful influence in worship and church building even in to the nineteenth century. Scholars have noted the influence of the scholarship of Christopher Wren and Bishop William Beveridge (who, in his *Synodikon*, a definitive edition of the canons of the early Church, showed himself a keen student of St Symeon of Thessalonike,[22] and was an ardent encourager of chancel screens; see Chapter 4 of this volume) traced the development of Temple motifs into the building of early Christian basilicas. Their studies in turn influenced the design of churches by Wren, Nicholas Hawksmoor, James Gibbs, and so on down through the next century.[23]

Conclusion

Theologically and architecturally, the assumptions of eighteenth-century church building could not seem farther from the priorities of our own day. Since then, among British architects, A. W. Pugin, with his passion for the chancel screen, may have been the last architect theologically literate enough to have been fully immersed in Patristic typology.[24] Even his illustrious counterpart at the other end of the Gothic Revival and designer of exquisite screens, Sir Ninian Comper, did not trace his influences back beyond the early Church, where he found the altar

Fig. 1: A Bible frontispiece of 1680. Angels rend the Veil to reveal the Holy of Holies of the Temple, where the sacrifice of the Day of Atonement (*Yom Kippur*) anticipates the Sacrifice of the Cross.

separated from the worshippers not 'by any choir but only by a very open screen, or merely by low *cancelli*'.[25]

The life of the contemporary Church has been cut off from some 1800 years of its worshipping life by a combination of architectural modernism and Critical Biblical theology. The ideology of architectural modernism assumes a clean break with the past both in terms of culture (including religion) and form. Although the theorists of the Liturgical Movement claimed that their aim was to 'return to the sources' of the

Fig. 2: Charles Wheatly, *A Rational Illustration of the Book of Common Prayer*, engraved plate by Michael Burghers, *c.*1668. The priest at the earthly altar offers the Eucharist in union with Christ at the heavenly altar. As Jeremy Taylor, Bishop of Down and Connor, summarised this theology, 'The church being the image of heaven, the priest the minister of Christ; the holy table being the copy of the celestial altar, and the eternal sacrifice of the lamb slain from the beginning of the world being always the same; it bleeds no more after the finishing of it on the cross, but it is wonderfully represented in heaven, and graciously represented here; by Christ's action there, by his commandment here.' (*The Worthy Communicant*, 1660)

Church's worship, this tended not to include the worship of the Temple. Peter Hammond, among the most influential of those writing on liturgy and architecture in Britain, did not mention it.[26] Louis Bouyer was a rare exception to this rule, but he was writing as a critical friend of the radical trajectory of developments the 1960s.[27]

Critical Biblical theory assumes that a unique 'original' meaning of Biblical texts can be discerned from historical and linguistic study, and that a typological understanding of Scripture has no place in this context. Furthermore, until recently scholars have neglected the Temple as a lens through which to interpret both the Old and New Testaments. Both of these movements cut off the Church and its worship from the past, and this has been evident in the re-ordering and building of new churches and in the Church's worship since the Second Vatican Council.

In the twenty-first century we find ourselves in a place where the certainties of modernism and a narrow historicist Biblical criticism no longer hold absolute sway. There is a greater degree of sympathetic understanding of historical forms of architecture, including screens, in their own contexts. A new generation of Biblical scholars, while not forgetting their critical disciplines, refuse to be confined by them and are rediscovering the truth to be found in traditional interpretations, including typology. Nevertheless, in most Anglican and Roman Catholic parishes which retain a eucharistic focus to their offering of worship, the assumptions and styles of the post-Vatican II mainstream remain the unexamined norm.[28] Worship remains focussed on the here and now; the Eucharist as the 'family meal of the Church' holds sway. Teaching on the eucharistic sacrifice and the Heavenly Temple is rare outside of conservative circles. It's difficult to imagine a movement to restore chancel screens to churches and worship any time soon.

Nevertheless, if the Church wants to be connected with its roots, if it wants to understand and appreciate fully the debt it owes to our Jewish brothers and sisters, if it wants to recapture something of that deeper and wider vision which might help it to move and grow beyond its present inward obsessions with divisive agendas, then it will have to begin to learn again the lessons of the Veil that unites even as it divides, that reveals that which it conceals. Christians are a people of Earth and Heaven, and in worship they pass from one to the other. The screen is a boundary between the two; it is a door that is always present but also always open, like the gates of the Heavenly City (Revelation 21:25). There are no easy solutions to our tensions, so we must remember the paradoxical reality of the double character of sacramental religion: the indivisibility of the material and immaterial, the visible and the invisible, the revealed and the concealed, the earthly and the heavenly. And then we might also begin to appreciate the contributions that screens, properly understood and used, can make to our worship and our faith.

Notes

1. A.W. Pugin, *A Treatise on Chancel Screens and Rood Lofts*, (1851) 3.
2. See Ivan Foletti and Katarína Kravčíková, *The Notion of Liminality and the Medieval Sacred Space* (Convivium Supplementum 3) (Turnhout, 2020).
3. I am indebted for the shape of this Biblical interpretation to N. T. Wright, 'Saving the World, Revealing the Glory: Atonement Then and Now', *ABC Religion and Ethics*, 12 April 2017: https://www.abc.net.au/religion/saving-the-world-revealing-the-glory-atonement-then-and-now/10095866.
4. See Margaret Barker, *Temple Theology: An Introduction*, (2004), 16–19.
5. Barker, *Temple Theology*, 29–30. See also Joan R. Branham, 'Penetrating the Sacred: Breaches and Barriers in the Jerusalem Temple', in Sharon E. J. Gerstel (ed.) *Thresholds of the Sacred: Architectural, Art Historical, Liturgical, and Theological Perspectives on Religious Screens, East and West*, (Washington, D.C., 2006), 20–22.
6. See the work of Margaret Barker, including *Temple Theology* and *Temple Themes in Christian Worship*, (2007).
7. John McDade, 'A promised fulfilled, a ransom paid', *The Tablet*, 8 October 2005, 6–7.
8. For a summary of these developments, with a helpful series of spatial reconstructions, see Peter Cobb, 'The Architectural Setting of the Liturgy', in Cheslyn Jones, Geoffrey Wainwright, Edward Yarnold, Paul Bradshaw (eds.), *The Study of Liturgy*, revised edition, (1992), 528–542.
9. See Barker, *Temple Themes*, ch. 7 and 8.
10. Basil Osborne, ' "For the Remissions of Sins": Eucharist and Atonement', The Constantinople Lecture 2004, *Koinonia*, New Series No. 54 (2008), 10–24.
11. Symeon of Thessalonike, *Interpretation of the Christian Temple and its Worship*, quoted in Nicholas P. Constas, 'Symeon of Thessalonike and the Theology of the Icon Screen', in Gerstel (ed.), *Thresholds of the Sacred*, 163– 183 (p. 167).
12. Guillaume Durand, *The Symbolism of Churches and Church Ornament:. A Translation of the First Book of the Rationale Divinorum Officiorum written by William Durandus*, (eds. John Mason Neale and Benjamin Webb), (1843) (New York, 1893), 15.
13. See William J. Hamblin and David Rolph Seely, *Solomon's Temple. Myth and History*, (2007), ch. 3.
14. Eamon Duffy, *The Stripping of the Altars: Traditional Religion in England 1400–1580*, (New Haven, 1992), 112. See 110–114 for his arguments on the accessibility of altar and Mass to the laity.
15. Jacqueline E. Jung, 'Beyond the Barrier: The Unifying Role of the Choir Screen in Gothic Churches', *The Art Bulletin*, 82, No. 4 (2000) 622–657, (p. 624); 'Seeing through Screens: The Gothic Choir Enclosure as a Frame', in Gerstel (ed.), *Thresholds of the Sacred*, 185–214.
16. See Jaime Lara, *City, Temple, Stage. Eschatological Architecture and Liturgical Theatrics in New Spain* (Notre Dame, 2004) ch. 4.

17. Achsah Guibbory, *Christian Identity, Jews and Israel in Seventeenth-Century England*, (Oxford, 2010), 20. For an exploration of seventeenth and early eighteenth-century Anglican use of Temple theology, see Peter Doll, 'The Architectural Expression of Primitive Christianity: William Beveridge and the Temple of Solomon', *Reformation & Renaissance Review* 13.2 (2011), 275–306.

18. Richard Hooker, *Of the Laws of Ecclesiastical Polity*, Bk v, ch.14, in *The Works of that Learned and Judicious Divine, Mr. Richard Hooker*, (ed. John Keble), (Oxford, 1865) II, 51–52.

19. This practice continued in use well into the nineteenth century: Walter Farquar Hook arranged the rebuilt Leeds Parish Church to accommodate communicants 'drawing near' at the invitation; see G. W. O. Addleshaw and Frederick Etchells, *The Architectural Setting of Anglican Worship*, (1948) 212–213. The practice was also illustrated in various devotional manuals and commentaries, most notably in the celebrated frontispiece to Charles Wheatly, *A Rational Illustration of the Book of Common Prayer*, (1722). See Peter Doll, *After the Primitive Christians: The Eighteenth-Century Anglican Eucharist in its Architectural Setting* (Cambridge, 1997).

20. Hooker, *Works*, V, xiv, 2, 53.

21. Joseph Mede, *The Reverence of God's House: A Sermon preached at St. Maries in Cambridge, before the Universitie on St Matthies day. Anno 1635/6*, (1638), 9–11.

22. William Beveridge, Συνοδικον, *sive pandectæ canonum ss. apostolorum, et conciliorum ab Ecclesia græca receptorum* (Oxford, 1672) II, Annotationes, 73.

23. See Doll, 'The Architectural Expression'; Pierre de la Ruffinière du Prey, *Hawksmoor's London Churches: Architecture and Theology* (Chicago, 2000); Vaughan Hart, *Nicholas Hawksmoor: Rebuilding Ancient Wonders* (New Haven, 2002); and more generally on this theme, Doll, *After the Primitive Christians*.

24. See *The Glossary of Ecclesiastical Ornament and Costume: compiled from Ancient Authorities and examples* (1844), iv–vii. The finest treatment of theological influences on Pugin is Christabel Powell, *Augustus Welby Pugin, designer of the British Houses of Parliament: The Victorian quest for a liturgical architecture* (Lewiston, 2006).

25. Ninian Comper, 'Of the Atmosphere of a Church', reprinted in Anthony Symondson and Stephen Bucknall, *Sir Ninian Comper* (Reading, 2006), 237.

26. Peter Hammond, *Liturgy and Architecture*, (1960).

27. Louis Bouyer, *Liturgy and Architecture*, (Notre Dame, 1967).

28. It remains to be seen what the impact on the wider Church might be of Pope Benedict XVI giving permission for the 'Extraordinary Rite' of the Mass, but his hope is that through the 'reform of the reform' the Ordinary and Extraordinary forms might mutually enrich one another. See Joseph Ratzinger, *The Spirit of the Liturgy* (San Francisco, 2000).

Chapter 2

Chancel Screens on the Eve of the Reformation

LUCY J. WRAPSON

England's medieval chancel or rood screens divided the nave from the chancel, the public part of the church from that of the priest; the earthly from the divine. Rather than acting as a practical physical barrier (they did not always have central doors) they functioned more as a spiritual one, providing a frame for the theatre of the Mass.[1] The earliest surviving parochial examples of these colourful, multivalent and multi-functional structures are thirteenth and fourteenth century in date.[2] By the late-fifteenth century, they were nigh on ubiquitous.

Rood screens were previously part of a larger varied ensemble of which much has been destroyed, specifically the great Crucifix (Rood), its flanking figures such as Mary and John the Evangelist (and sometimes the good and bad thieves), all of which formerly stood on the rood loft or were suspended over it (Fig. 1). Only a very few Roods or fragments of them have survived the Reformation, all of them are separated from their original context. Rather more lofts survive; St Mary's, Attleborough (Norfolk), St Edith's, Coates by Stow (Lincolnshire), and St Mary's, Atherington (Devon) being some examples. It is, however, necessary to look to Brittany or to Sir Ninian Comper's restored screens at St Peter and St Paul, Eye, or St John the Baptist's, Lound, in Suffolk to help imagine what England's once colourful and elaborate screens might have looked like with their sculptures and parapets intact.[3]

With one or two exceptions, these structures were not termed 'screens' until the seventeenth century, following the removal of their Roods and lofts, a term likely to derive from un-lofted domestic partitions. In contemporary late-medieval records, they were known as rood lofts, perkes, sollers, pulpita, allures, and candlebeams.[4] These terms varied according to each English region, but they habitually referenced the gallery or loft, since taken down. The original terminology emphasises the importance of the upper gallery and its access to the Rood. Reformation period dismantling means that no single term fully conveys both what is left now and what was intended originally. In this article, I therefore use the term 'rood screen', a nineteenth-century

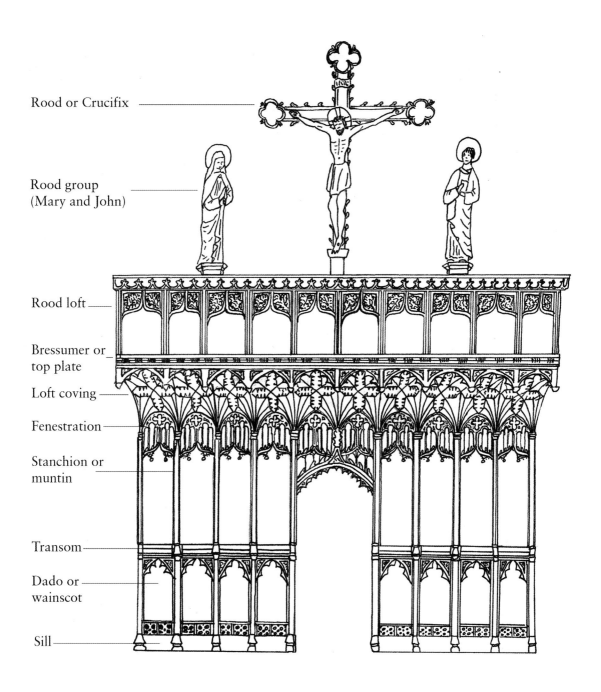

Fig. 1: Drawing showing the constituent parts of an East Anglian rood screen and their names.
(© Hamilton Kerr Institute, University of Cambridge)

confection popularised during the 1848 rood-screen controversy, and the term 'chancel screen', which suggests a purpose to screen the chancel, interchangeably, acknowledging the problems with both.

Two English regions are known for retaining the largest numbers of screens, both painted and now stripped of their original paint, East Anglia, particularly the county of Norfolk and the West Country, specifically the county of Devon. There are other regions with significant numbers of extant screens, notably on both sides of the border in the Welsh Marches.[5] The prevalence of often retro-fitted rood loft stairs in now-screenless medieval churches from Cumberland to Cornwall is a testament to their near ubiquity by the late Middle Ages. Although there are compelling reasons why the West Country and East Anglia might have had large numbers of screens by the fifteenth century (wealth leading to widespread later medieval church building and rebuilding perhaps being one), the survival of pre-Reformation screenwork can be as much to do with their post-Reformation treatment as anything. In a particularly well-documented case, within ten years, between 1727 and 1737, 71 medieval screens were taken down in Yorkshire, leaving that county with few surviving screens, despite noteworthy examples at St Michael and All Angels, Hubberholme and St Oswald's, Flamborough.[6]

Identifying Tudor screens

Is it possible to establish what constitutes a surviving English screen on the 'eve of the Reformation'? The answer for the region I have personally studied most, East Anglia is yes. Nonetheless, establishing a secure chronology for East Anglian screens is complex.[7] Some dates can be found inscribed on screens, in records of inscriptions collected by antiquaries, in wills bequeathing money to their creation, and in churchwardens' accounts. With all these strands of data taken together, there is dating evidence for about 20 percent of screens in East Anglia, with greater or lesser precision depending on the source.[8] Dating Devon's screens is hampered by the loss of its historical wills in the bombing of its record office in the Second World War, although it is thought few pre-Reformation wills survived in any case.[9] Despite this, its approximately 140 screens can be examined in the light of twelve dated examples (about 9 percent of surviving screens).[10]

By relating this framework to aspects of construction and painting, which I have done for East Anglian screens, it is possible then to group stylistically-related works around existing dates, even to the extent of identifying the work of specific workshops of both carpentry and painting.[11] This approach is, however, not without its difficulties and uncertainties. As chancel screens were large, expensive, composite structures, they were often the product of parish fundraising and could take decades to complete.[12] Where screens are dated by painted inscription, this marks the end of a long story of construction and decoration, which were separate processes involving distinct craftsmen. This separation of the crafts is indicated by the habitual presence of barbs of paint (known as 'mahlrands') which indicate that rood screens were painted once they had been constructed, as well as by the identifiable outputs of both carpentry and painting workshops which rarely overlap.[13]

As I have explored elsewhere,[14] a significant change in woodworking technique helps the dating of screens and can also assist in dating undated examples. Charles Tracy and Hugh Harrison were first to note a change in carpentry jointing techniques in continental woodworking in their study of choir stalls at Amiens Cathedral.[15] Following that, Tim Howson in his 2009 study of the woodwork of Suffolk screens noted that there are two main approaches to jointing the junction between transom and stanchion on fifteenth and sixteenth-century perpendicular style screens in East Anglia.[16] After surveying about 40 Norfolk and Suffolk screens and comparing them to known and dated will bequests, he concluded that mason's mitre joints, an earlier joint type, were superseded by scribed joints and that this reflected an innovation in technique on the continent as described by Tracy and Harrison.

I have since compiled about a hundred examples of dated screens and their transom jointing methods via site visits in East Anglia (Fig. 2). This work has confirmed that the scribed transom to stanchion joint was first used in the 1480s and was used invariably after 1505. The period from c.1480 until c.1500 was one where both jointing techniques were used, as well as a hybridised version of the two, with the scribed joint finding increasing favour (though mason's mitre joints did continue to be used). The earliest dated scribed joint I have found dates to 1474, but it is by c.1485 that they became more widespread.[17]

The significance of this is that an undated East Anglian screen with scribed joints is likely to have been made c.1485–1536. This transition coincides with the beginning of the Tudor period and so a study of scribe-jointed screens and their painted schemes is effectively a study of screens on the eve of the Reformation. It is clear from screens in other parts of England that this change happened elsewhere, although at what date and through what route is uncertain. As the work of Harrison and West has shown, these technical changes also came about in the West Country where there are also both mason's mitre and scribe-jointed

screens.[18] When Devon's scribe-jointed screens are examined closely in terms of other characteristics such as their carpentry and painting style, it is credible that they too date from the late fifteenth through to the sixteenth century.

Fig. 2: Rood screen transom joints: Ranworth, Norfolk (mason's mitre, dated c.1479), and Southwold, Suffolk (scribed, dated c.1500–10). Note the difference in where the joint appears on the front of the transom in each case.
(© Hamilton Kerr Institute, University of Cambridge)

Iconographic, material and stylistic characteristics of Tudor-period screens

Having established how to identify a relevant body of surviving screens, this paper now concentrates on figurative screens of the Tudor period, that is on scribed-jointed screens dating from around 1485 until the Reformation, and on those hybrid and mason's mitre-jointed screens with Tudor period will-bequest dates.[19] I first compare Plantagenet and Tudor period screens to see whether there are any definable differences. While this effort concentrates on East Anglian screens, I also demonstrate some of the regional differences still discernible between parochial chancel screens in England, particularly in terms of continental stylistic influences.

Once the compartmentalised perpendicular style screen had been developed in the early fifteenth century, its iconography and decoration followed quite clearly defined patterns and traditions, as exemplified by the rood screen at St James', Castle Acre (Norfolk), which probably dates to *c*.1420–40.[20] The Apostles were the earliest figures represented on the lower reaches or dados of screens, likely because of an overall change in the association of the lower parts of the chancel screen with the great Rood and especially with themes of the Passion, judgement and redemption, connected vertically to the Last Judgement in the form of a chancel arch wall painting or wooden tympanum. At St Michael's, Irstead (Norfolk), the fourteenth-century screen bears two designs, one earlier than the other. Infrared photography makes more visible an underlying crown of thorns design on the screen, which has been updated to depict the Apostles, likely in the fifteenth century. At All Saints, Edingthorpe (Norfolk), a decorative scheme was also later updated to depict an apocopated Apostle-set of six saints. Many of the earlier subdivided screens were seemingly designed with twelve compartments in order to carry the Apostles.

Yet by the time that figurative painting became common practice on screen dados by the mid-fifteenth century, there was flexibility as to who was represented, and screens could swell to hold more figures. Eamon Duffy has written extensively on the subject of saints on rood screens, and on the patronage affecting their selection, comparing Devon and East Anglia. He concludes that the guiding principle behind the popularity of certain saints, specifically virgin martyrs and other helper saints, on late medieval screens was their intercessory role.[21] Saints such as St Anne might be invoked to aid fecundity, or St Apollonia in the management or prevention of toothache, and they were very approachable for the laity, sited as they were on the western face of the lower part of the screen. Other figures could appear too, such as kings and prophets.[22] I have argued elsewhere that the choice of saints on the screen at St Mary's, North Tuddenham reflects the fact that plague was endemic in that area at the date it was made.[23] The subject matter of screens might also reflect the distribution of the congregation in front of it as at St Mary's, North Elmham or St Helen's, Ranworth (Norfolk) and St Andrew's, Westhall (Suffolk) where female saints grace the north range and male saints the south, mirroring the segregation of the genders in church. The screen at Ranworth is unusual in being one of those examples where the tradition was inverted, as the women's side appears to have been the south side of the church where the nave altar was dedicated to the Holy Kinship.[24]

East Anglian screens were carved and constructed in oak, with at least some of the carving being finished *in situ*. Oak was often of two grades, local and imported. The imported wood was usually straight-grained Baltic boards and the bigger beams were more erratically grained local wood. Once the work of the carpenters was complete, the screen was painted as and when funds permitted. Although many screens have now been stripped of their original paint, fragments of paint have been found on all but a couple of the hundreds of screens in the East Anglian region.

The painting of screens from *c*.1400 until the beginning of the Tudor period followed a fairly standard model, with slight variations or signature features found between different workshops. Screens were usually covered with a white chalk ground, bound in animal glue, sometimes followed by a lead-white priming and subsequent layers in drying oil. The mullions and upper fenestration were often painted in white, red and green and gilded, and the mouldings framing the dado panels decorated with floral patterns and barber's pole decoration. Blue pigments were used for the canopy of the loft, which in surviving examples is star-studded or angel-bedecked.[25]

Under-drawing was usually undertaken using a carbon black medium. The backgrounds of the figure panels were decorated alternately in copper green and vermilion and these were in turn decorated with stencils in gold and sometimes silver leaf, which is typically now tarnished to black. Figure painting was usually fairly calligraphic in tone, with flesh paint outlined in brown or black. The limited modelling of form was often done in highlights and glazes over mid-tones. A repeat casting method known as 'tin relief' was fairly commonly used in East Anglia, but is not found on the more intricately carved Devon screens.

East Anglian Tudor-period screens have much the same structure, and broadly the same materials and handling of ornamental detailing, as their predecessors. However, during the fifteenth and sixteenth centuries, England was very open to artistic influence especially from France, the Low Countries and Rhine, both from imported works of art and imported artists. This influence came to be reflected in both the iconography and style of painting on rood screens by *c*.1500, as can be seen at Wiggenhall St Mary the Virgin (Norfolk; Fig. 3).

Both Devon and East Anglia were influenced according to their respective geographical positions. Devon had an influx of Breton craftsmen responsible for screens, as both surviving screens and written evidence indicates.[26] The influence of Breton craftsmen and design

Fig. 3: St Catherine of Alexandria and St Barbara from the south side of the rood screen at Wiggenhall St Mary the Virgin, Norfolk. The saints stand in front of the kind of wall seen on northern European altarpieces of the same period. (© Hamilton Kerr Institute, University of Cambridge)

spread wider than the presence of craftsmen and can be seen too in the incidental detail of West Country screens made by English craftsmen.

East Anglia's deep involvement with the cloth trade led to significant cultural influence from the Low Countries including the Burgundian Netherlands and Rhineland. Charles Tracy and Hugh Harrison have convincingly demonstrated the Spring chantry in St Peter and St Paul, Lavenham (Suffolk), to be Flemish influenced, in their view perhaps the work of second generation immigrants.[27] Thomas Spring III was himself a wealthy clothier and his chantry chapel screen demonstrates his taste for continental influenced design (Fig. 4). Antwerp was a leading centre for artistic production and export. By the early sixteenth century, records show that numerous small-scale ready-made works of art were imported into England including books of hours and altarpieces.

Towards the latter end of the pre-Reformation period, from around 1500, a discernible shift in design appears to have taken place, powerfully influenced by continental print sources and the new style we have come to term 'Renaissance'. Landscape and ideas of recessional space became an increasing factor in panel compositions, and narrative scenes rather

Fig. 4: The Flemish-influenced chantry chapel of Thomas Spring III, St Peter and St Paul, Lavenham, Suffolk. (Photo: Mark Kirby)

than iconic saints increased in popularity. This interest in landscape also came about on West Country screens, as evident at St Manarch's, Lanreath (Cornwall). Devon is also notable for its adoption of Classical motifs – in several cases, female sybils are to be found depicted on the dados of screens.[28]

Screen designers and carpenters accommodated for this by widening the dado panels, and sometimes no longer subdividing them, as can be seen on the screen at St Andrew's, Wellingham (Norfolk; Fig. 5).

Fig. 5: St Michael depicted on the south side of the rood screen at St Andrew's, Wellingham, Norfolk. (© Hamilton Kerr Institute, University of Cambridge)

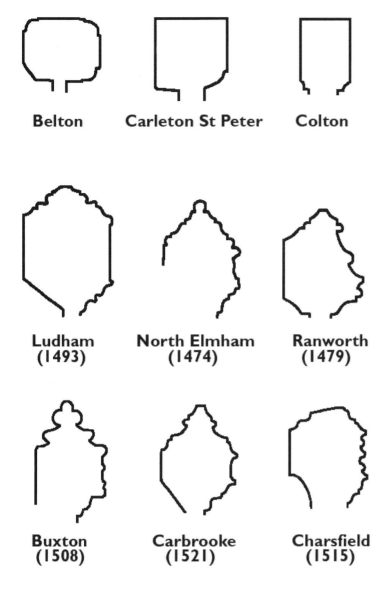

Fig. 6: Three periods of transom cross-sectional moulding profiles on East Anglian screens. In the top row are those of fourteenth-century date, noted from the style of the screens. In the middle are mid-late fifteenth-century examples, and in the bottom row are the sixteenth-century examples. The dates are either inscribed dates or averaged will bequest dates. Not to scale. (© Hamilton Kerr Institute, University of Cambridge)

Belton   **Carleton St Peter**   **Colton**

Ludham   **North Elmham**   **Ranworth**
(1493)   **(1474)**   **(1479)**

Buxton   **Carbrooke**   **Charsfield**
(1508)   **(1521)**   **(1515)**

Taking just one element of the structure of screens – the transom rail cross-sectional shape – it is easy to visualise change in design over time (Fig. 6). The simple square-sectioned transom rails of the fourteenth century gave way to the polygonal design of perpendicular screens in the fifteenth. There was then a trend towards screen dados becoming larger and more complex into the sixteenth century.

Influence came directly from abroad through the copying of continental prints. Byam Shaw first noted that two saints – Peter and Andrew – on the screen at St Mary's, Worstead (Norfolk) were derived from prints by Martin Schongauer, likely through copies such as those

Fig. 7: St Sebastian, painted as a likeness of Henry VII, on the screen at St Mary's, North Tuddenham, Norfolk. (© Hamilton Kerr Institute, University of Cambridge)

by Israhel van Meckenem. John Mitchell later noted that the St Simon on the Worstead screen derived from a Lucas van Leyden St Peter.[29] The Lucas van Leyden Apostle series dates to *c*.1510, the Worstead screen is dated 1512 and must have appeared strikingly contemporary when new. The two surviving panels at Tacolneston (Norfolk) were identified by Strange and Mitchell respectively as having derived from Lucas van Leyden and Monogrammist FVB.[30]

Once print sources became popular as an inspiration or guide for panel composition, the use of alternating green and red backgrounds adorned with stencils declined, replaced instead by landscapes or gilded cloths of honour. Where red and green stencilled backgrounds were retained, they were turned into cloths of honour, sometimes held by angels behind the saints. By the sixteenth century, there are even instances of portraiture on screens, as at North Tuddenham, where the figure of St Sebastian is painted in a likeness of Henry VII (Fig. 7).

As well as changes in painting style, there were some commensurate alterations in painting technique on late-medieval screens. This mainly manifests itself in the increased use of modelling, as can be seen when comparing figures from the rood screens at All Saints, Carleton Rode (Norfolk) and St Andrew's, Bramfield (Suffolk; Fig. 8). This change can even be seen within the same workshop when comparing the handling of St Philip's basket of bread at Ranworth, Norfolk and on the later screen at St Edmund's, Southwold (Suffolk). Both instances demonstrate artists' newfound interests in depicting recessional space and a more naturalistic depiction of light.

Duffy has demonstrated that the most active years for rood loft building were between 1490 and 1520 based on Norfolk and Suffolk will bequests.[31] In his view, the slight reduction in bequests between 1520 and 1540 more likely indicates that by this date most churches had completed the construction and decoration of their screens rather than being a sign of impending reform.

The impact of Reformation on medieval rood lofts

The dissolution officially sanctioned the destruction, dismantling and sometimes sale of the fittings of monastic churches, including screens and lofts.[32] From 1536, cult images in conventual and parochial settings were also targeted for destruction.[33] Despite this, the building of parochial rood lofts continued well into the reign of Henry VIII as shown by documentary and physical remains, for example at Wellingham (Norfolk) where the screen is inscribed with the date 1532. A large bequest was left by a John Jamys to make the rood loft as late as

Fig. 8: Rood screen panel, St Simon, c.1460, oil on panel, Carleton Rode, Norfolk compared with St Matthew, c.1500, oil on panel, Bramfield, Suffolk. (© Hamilton Kerr Institute, University of Cambridge)

1538 in St Mary's, Banham (Norfolk).[34] Records show that rood lofts were made as late as 1546 in the case of St Andrew's, East Allington (Devon). The makers of the screen at Atherington sought redress for a lack of payment for their early 1540s work through the chancery courts between 1544 and 1547.[35]

While the 1536 Royal Injunctions had criticised the cult of images, relics and pilgrimage, those two years later were more forceful, forbidding both pilgrimage and outward manifestations of devotion to the dead and to the cult of saints.[36] However, tapers and candles were still permitted to be burnt before the Rood and there was to be no officially sanctioned destruction of the Rood or any part of its supporting structure at that date, although attacks did take place between 1538 and 1540.[37] By the death of Henry VIII in January 1547, pilgrimage sites, the shrines of saints and the entire monastic system had been taken apart.[38] The building of rood lofts had slowed in pace, and those in the monastic setting had been destroyed or sold.

It was under Edward VI (1547–53) that the building of lofts halted, images were attacked, and Roods were burnt. The Injunctions of 1547 led to Royal Visitations from September.[39] The Visitations led to the destruction of many images, but the distinction between a used and a misused image was not clarified until the end of 1547. The official order to remove all images from London came first, and was extended by Cranmer to the rest of the country in February 1548.[40] All images were to be removed from churches and destroyed and the campaign of destruction lasted many years. By 1550, ownership of religious images would lead to fines and imprisonment.[41]

The destruction of Roods and rood groups by iconoclasts was so successful that only five or so fragments of British Roods have survived. Rood beams, like the one at St Mary's, Tunstead (Norfolk) are more common in their survival, although where figurative, they too suffered destruction; a sole surviving Golgotha rood beam remains in St Andrew's, Cullompton (Devon). Under Edward VI, screens themselves were retained and acquired a new function. Where the Rood and its attendant figures had once stood, Royal Arms were now positioned.[42] However, it was not until the reign of Elizabeth I that rood lofts, in the modern understanding of the term – the parapets – were officially condemned. Clearly in a time of great turmoil and without official sanction, some reformers such as Bishop Hooper in 1551–52, sought and succeeded in the abolition of some rood lofts.[43]

Some Roods, rood lofts and tympana were restored during the Catholic reign of Mary (1553–58). An example can be found at St Catherine's, Ludham (Norfolk), where the chancel arch tympanum was put back after its discovery in the rood stair in 1879.[44] Also present at Ludham, now on the chancel side of the arch, is an Elizabethan Royal Arms on canvas, used to cover the tympanum during Elizabeth's reign and after. The wooden tympanum is pre-Reformation in date and has two or more phases of painting, one likely Marian in date.[45] The figure of Christ and the Cross has been crudely added over blank space on the tympanum previously hidden by statuary of the same subject. This tympanum must have survived the 1540s, in the hope that it would one day be put back; it was modified in Mary's reign and then covered up during Elizabeth's.

1559 was a year of widespread image destruction, both of new images created during Mary's reign and of the earlier examples that had re-emerged from hiding. The Elizabethan Order of 10 October 1561 made it explicit that the partition between the nave and the chancel was to be kept, but for the first time, rood lofts were ordered to be removed.[46]

Despite the orders to remove both, some Roods and rood lofts must have survived into the seventeenth century as both the 28 August, 1643 Ordinance and May, 1644 Ordinance explicitly state their prohibition.[47] Determining the date of iconoclastic damage such as the scratching of eyes and destruction of prayer clauses is, however, rarely possible.[48]

Conclusion

The technical study, specifically of carpentry joints, shows that Tudor screens, those on the eve of the Reformation, can be identified with a degree of certainty, due to a construction change in rood screen manufacture in East Anglia. This same change is observed elsewhere in England, although at present does not have the dating evidence tied to the physical evidence. Between 1485 and 1538 screen production was widespread and well-established. Screen painting in the Tudor period can be seen to be both continuing a well-worn tradition, technically and iconographically and capable of adopting the latest continental fashions.

However, the Reformation's religious turmoil meant that rood lofts such as St Andrew's, North Burlingham, finished only in 1536, were probably defaced just ten years later, and their lofts and Roods destroyed. The making of rood screens ceased from the accession of Edward VI, and extensive dismantling, deliberate whitewashing and widespread iconoclasm likely dates from this period. A brief Catholic revivalist period under Mary between 1553 and 1558, is perhaps best exemplified in East Anglia at Ludham and by screen at Hubberholme (Yorkshire) which is dated 1558 and was signed by its carpenter, William Jake. In both cases, craftsmen mended what was already present or locally scavenged, perhaps from the Premonstratensian monastery at Coverham Abbey. Hubberholme's loft is earlier in date than the parts Jake constructed and signed and Ludham saw the addition of a painted cross where a sculpted one previously stood. Many parishes lacked the means to replace Roods, lofts and screens and many sculptures were replaced by cheap canvas at this time. Within the span of a couple of decades, it appears that the craft structures and traditions of rood screen carpentry and painting were fractured beyond repair.

Notes

1. For more on this see J. Jung, 'Seeing through screens, the Gothic enclosure as frame', in S. Gerstel (ed.), *Thresholds of the Sacred*, (Dumbarton Oaks, 2006), 185–213; J. Jung, 'Beyond the barrier: the unifying role of the choir screen in Gothic churches', *Art Bulletin*, 82 (2000), 622–57.

2. A. Vallance, *English Church Screens*, (1936), 31–47; F. Bond, *Screens and Galleries in English Churches*, (1908), 87–93.

3. For Brittany see Y. Pelletier, *Les jubés de Bretagne*, (Ouest-France, 1986). For Eye see A. Baker, *English Panel Paintings 1400–1558: A survey of figure paintings on East Anglian rood-screens*, (2011), 138–9.

4. Vallance, *English Church Screens*, 31–2. For 'aler', see E. Hobhouse, *Church-wardens' accounts of Croscombe, Pilton, Patton, Tintinhull, Morebath, and St. Michael's, Bath, ranging from A.D. 1349 to 1560*, (1890), 79, 88, 92, 93, 95.

5. R. Wheeler, *The Medieval Church Screens of the Southern Marches*, (Little Logaston, 2006).

6. Vallance, *English Church Screens*, 91 cites C. R. Norcliffe's 1862 paper for the *Yorkshire Architectural Society*.

7. I have published a more detailed version of this methodology in L. Wrapson, 'Towards new methodological approaches for examining rood screens', in S. Bucklow, R. Marks and L. Wrapson (eds.), *The Art and Science of the Church Screen in Medieval Europe: Making, Meaning, Preserving*, (Woodbridge, 2016), 45–70.

8. *Ibid.*

9. For the destruction of the record office see https://swheritage.org.uk/devon-archives/visit/local-studies-library/. However, Devon wills from the Prerogative Court at Canterbury have survived, and a sample 97 out of 626 were read by M. A. Williams in the course of his doctorate on Devon screens, yielding six references to West Country screens, two of which are extant: M. A. Williams, 'Medieval English Roodscreens with Special Reference to Devon', (doctoral thesis, University of Exeter, 2008).

10. L. Wrapson and E. Sinclair, 'The polychromy of Devon screens: preliminary analytical results', in Bucklow *et al* (eds.), *The Church Screen*, 150–174, esp. 155.

11. This is dealt with in my PhD Thesis: L. J. Wrapson, 'Patterns of Production: A Technical Art Historical Study of East Anglia's Late Medieval Screens', (doctoral thesis, University of Cambridge, 2013). It will also be the subject of my forthcoming book.

12. Much of the dating is underpinned by the following work: S. Cotton, 'Mediæval roodscreens in Norfolk – their construction and painting dates', *Norfolk Archaeology*, 40: 1, (1987), 44–54; P. Northeast, 'Suffolk churches in the late middle ages: the evidence of wills', in C. Harper-Bill, Carole Rawcliffe and R. Wilson (eds.), *East Anglia's History: Studies in Honour of Norman Scarfe*, (Woodbridge, 2002), 93-106; P. Northeast (ed.), *Wills of the Archdeaconry of Sudbury 1439–1474: Wills from the Register 'Baldewyne'. Pt 1: 1439–61*, (Woodbridge, 2001); P. Northeast and H. Falvey (eds.), *Wills of the Archdeaconry of Sudbury 1439–1474: Wills from the Register 'Baldewyne'. Pt 2: 1461–1474*, (Woodbridge, 2010); S. Cotton, H. Lunnon and L. Wrapson, 'Medieval rood screens in Suffolk: their construction and painting dates', *Proceedings of the Suffolk Institute for Archaeology and History*, 43, Part 2 (2014), 219–234. For example, at Cawston in Norfolk, the first known bequest to the screen is in 1460 and the last in 1507, and a range of different painters from different workshops were involved (in my view four).

13. Wrapson, 'Patterns of Production'.

14. Wrapson, 'Towards new methodological approaches for examining rood screens'.

15. C. Tracy and H, Harrison, *The Choir-Stalls of Amiens Cathedral*, (Reading, 2004).

16. T. Howson, 'Suffolk church screens: their production in the late middle ages and their conservation today', (PG Dip in Building Conservation, Architectural Association, 2009), 2 vols., vol. 1, 42, Fig. 4.6.

17. The antiquarian Blomefield's notebooks reveal that there was previously a date of 1474 inscribed on the doors of the North Elmham screen (I am grateful to David King for finding and passing on this information). The date was not transcribed into Blomefield's published volume.

18. H. Harrison and J. West, 'West Country rood screens: construction and practice', in Bucklow *et al* (eds.), *The Church Screen*, 123–149.

19. I have explored screens of the Tudor period in the following publication: L. J. Wrapson, 'A Medieval Context for the Artistic Production of Painted Surfaces in England: Evidence from East Anglia (*c.*1400–50)', in T. Cooper, A. Burnstock, M. Howard and E. Town (eds.), *Painting in Britain 1500–1630, Production, Influences and Patronage*, (2015), 166–175.

20. Wrapson, 'Patterns of Production', 555. Baker, following Pevsner, dates it to *c.*1400. Baker, *English Panel Paintings*, 129–30.

21. E. Duffy, 'The parish, piety and patronage in late medieval East Anglia: the evidence of screens', in K. French, G. Gibbs and B. Kümin (eds.), *The Parish in English Life, 1400–1600*, (Manchester, 1997), 133–62; E. Duffy, 'Holy Maydens, Holy Wyfes: the Cult of Women Saints in Fifteenth- and Sixteenth-century England', in W. J. Sheils and D. Wood (eds.), *Women in the Church: papers read at the 1989 Summer Meeting and the 1990 Winter Meeting of the Ecclesiastical History Society*, (Oxford and Cambridge), 175–96.

22. J. Luxford 'Sacred kingship, genealogy and the late medieval rood screen: Catfield and beyond', in Bucklow *et al* (eds.), *The Church Screen, 101–122.*

23. This article will form part of a forthcoming festschrift.

24. M. Naydenova Slade, 'Images of the Holy kinship in England, *c*.1170 to *c*.1525', (doctoral thesis, Courtauld Institute of Art, London, 2008), 148–50.

25. Visible still at St Andrew's, Bramfield, Suffolk and All Saints', Tilbrook, Cambridgeshire (formerly Hunts).

26. J. Allan, 'Breton woodworkers in the immigrant communities of south-west England, 1500–1550', *Post-Medieval Archaeology*, 48, No.2 (2014), 320–56.

27. C. Tracy, C. and H. Harrison, 'Thomas Spring's Chantry and Parclose at Lavenham, Suffolk', *Journal of the British Archaeological Association*, 164, (2011), 221–59.

28. A. Baker, 'Representations of Sibyls on Rood-screens in Devon', *Report and Transactions of the Devonshire Association*, 136 (2004), 71–97.

29. J. Mitchell, 'Painting in East Anglia around 1500: the continental connection', in J. Mitchell (ed.), *England and the Continent in the Middle Ages: studies in memory of Andrew Martindale*, (Stamford, 2000), 365–80.

30. Mitchell 'Painting in East Anglia around 1500', 376; and E. F. Strange, 'Notes on the rood-screen in Tacolneston church, Norfolk', *Proceedings of the Society of Antiquaries of London*, Second series, 19 (1903), 142–6.

31. Duffy, 'The parish, piety and patronage', 138.

32. I have published an extended version of this section of the paper in L. Wrapson, 'East Anglian medieval church screens. A brief guide to their physical history', *Bulletin of the Hamilton Kerr Institute*, 4 (2013), 33–47.

33. M. Aston, *England's Iconoclasts, vol. 1, Laws against Images*, (Oxford, 1988), 225.

34. Cotton, 'Mediæval roodscreens in Norfolk', 46.

35. The National Archives (K), C1/1116.

36. E. Duffy, *The Stripping of the Altars: Traditional Religion in England 1400–1580*, (New Haven and London, 1992), 407.

37. Vallance, *English Church Screens*, 5.

38. R. Deacon and P. Lindley, *Image and Idol: Medieval Sculpture*, (2001), 33.

39. Duffy, *The Stripping of the Altars*, 448–77.

40. R. Marks, *Image and Devotion in Late Medieval England*, (Stroud 2004), 263–4.

41. *Ibid.*

42. Only a single set of Edwardian royal arms survives, at Westerham, Kent. D. MacCulloch, *Tudor Church Militant. Edward VI and the Protestant Reformation*, (1999), 16.

43. Vallance, *English Church Screens*, 77.

44. P. Mortlock and C. V. Roberts, *The Guide to Norfolk Churches*, (Cambridge, 2007), 179. The royal arms, which must have historically covered the wooden tympanum, is on canvas and was placed in its current position, facing east, on a new stretcher in the 1970s. I am grateful to Pauline Plummer for this information.

45. From the ground there appear to be two schemes, but it cannot be ruled out that a close examination may reveal more layers or campaigns.

46. Vallance, *English Church Screens*, 86.

47. J. Spraggon, *Puritan Iconoclasm in the English Civil War*, (Woodbridge, 2003), 79.
48. T. Cooper (ed.), *The Journal of William Dowsing: Iconoclasm in East Anglia during the English Civil War*, (Woodbridge, 2001), 106. Citing Weever's 1631 reference to damage to brasses, Cooper concludes that prayer clause mutilation cannot therefore be taken as a conclusive evidence of 1640s iconoclasm.

Chapter 3

'A comely partition betwixt the chancel and the church': English Chancel Screens from Elizabeth I to the Civil War

TREVOR COOPER

There is a common misunderstanding that pre-Reformation screens were taken down as part of a general programme of iconoclasm after Elizabeth came to the throne in November 1558.[1]

Tilney All Saints in Norfolk (Fig. 1) tells a rather different story. For here is a *new* chancel screen (or 'partition' as contemporaries would have called it) being built in 1618 to replace the medieval one, which was then set aside in an aisle. There was of course no crucifix (or 'Rood') above this new screen nor any loft to hold candles and images. Its top – which may perhaps be the original rood beam cased in with new work – looks incomplete; but, like many other screens of this date, it originally carried the Royal Arms and strapwork cresting (Fig. 2b), both of which now hang on a nearby wall. The chancel may well have been used for the communion service, a common though not universal practice.[2]

Fig. 1: The chancel at Tilney All Saints, Norfolk, looking north-west. The chancel screen (left) is dated 1618. The parclose screen on the north is medieval, as are the stalls. The desks are Victorian.

Whilst Roods did come down early in Elizabeth's reign, and so did (more slowly) the rood lofts, most people in England would have worshipped in a church with a chancel partition, usually the surviving medieval one. It is in subsequent centuries that the majority of screens were lost.

This chapter begins by exploring the survival of pre-Reformation screens in parish churches. It then looks at those chancel partitions which were newly built during our eighty-year period, drawing on an extended Annex which considers in detail the fourteen new screens which carry dates. Finally, it uses two case studies to ask whether a richly ornamented screen tells us anything about the theological motivation of those paying for it.

The survival of screens

Queen Elizabeth's settlement of religion followed the Edwardian Reformation of ten years earlier in taking a negative view of images and altars, following the Swiss (rather than Lutheran) approach to church interiors, although in practice much figurative stained glass remained intact. Although from the early seventeenth century there was some re-introduction of imagery into parish churches, this remained rare and controversial.

In England, screens had been criticised for some time, including by such influential early reformers as Martin Bucer and John Hooper. In a sermon before King Edward VI in March 1550, Hooper had made the theological point that having the minister in his normal place in the chancel whilst the congregation were in the nave 'separateth the congregation of Christ one from the other, as though the veil and partition of the temple in the old law yet should remain in the church'. Furthermore, removing the separation would 'cause the people the better to understand the things read there by the minister', a practical consideration related to the theological imperative for everyone to understand what the minister was saying. Hooper had experienced such worship in Zurich, where the congregation received communion seated in the nave facing a communion table, behind which were the presiding minister and elders, speaking in the vernacular.[3]

Despite this, there had been no general removal of screens in the Edwardian period, and only a very limited removal of rood lofts.[4] Thus for some reformers the Elizabethan re-introduction of Protestantism provided an opportunity to deal once and for all not only with Roods and rood lofts (as focii of devotion) but also with screens (as symbolic and practical barriers).

On screens they were to be disappointed. The Royal Commissioners who traversed the country in 1559 ensuring clergy subscribed to the new regime also required that churches remove altars and images, including the Rood; but they paid little attention to the loft, and none to the screen, on which they had no instructions. More radical reform took place the following year in London, where, with the encouragement of Bishop Grindal, the lofts (but not screens) came down. Some enthusiastic churches in Essex followed suit.[5]

To maintain control, the Privy Council issued a Royal Order on 10 October 1561 (see Appendix). For the first time it was made explicit that rood lofts were to be removed and replaced by a 'convenient crest' on the upper beam. However screens were to stay, or be replaced if already removed, to ensure 'a comely partition betwixt the chancel and the church'. Like much else in the early days of Elizabeth's reign – such as the Prayer Book requirement, unique in Europe, that the minister should celebrate communion facing not east or west, but south – the Order appears to be a compromise: in this case, removing those features attracting devotion whilst minimising disruptive change.

Following the Order, in the south of England rood lofts were removed reasonably quickly, though a number of parishes required what Ronald Hutton called 'serious pressure' from diocesan officials, and in some cases it took years to enforce compliance. The very limited evidence for the north of England suggests little removal of lofts until after the appointment of Grindal as Archbishop of York (1570–75).[6] But come down they eventually did.

In contrast, chancel screens are only rarely recorded as being taken down. However, over the next couple of decades the reformers did largely achieve their wish not to separate the minister from his people, as bishops encouraged the minister to read the regular Sunday service from the nave, not the chancel. In future years the chancel was increasingly used for congregational seating to accommodate a growing population and the desire to maintain a single space for minister and people probably explains why many medieval screens were cut down to form a partition about the same height as a box pew. Very often the work is not recorded, so it is not known when in the last four hundred years this typically took place.[7]

So medieval screens largely remained in place. They might be tidied up where they had lost their vaulting, and images of saints on the dado were painted over or defaced or both (literally defaced – though the term was applied generally to pre-Reformation devotional items, to mean 'spoil' or 'disfigure').[8] Biblical texts were sometimes painted

Fig. 2: Examples of cresting. 2a (*top left*): St Peter & St Paul, Swalcliffe, Oxfordshire, early modern cresting once above the medieval screen; the hymnbooks give scale. 2b (*top right*): Tilney All Saints, Norfolk, old and damaged photo (here digitally enhanced). 2c (*bottom left*): St Lawrence's, Folke, Dorset, screen probably of about the same date as the church (1628), since altered. The large pointed arches are unusual. 2d (*bottom right*): St Mary's, Longworth, Oxfordshire, date of screen unknown.

on the screen, either on the dado or along the upperwork, but only a few examples survive, and we do not know how often this was done. Surviving texts on medieval screens do not relate to the function of the screen nor the chancel behind it – the screen is simply a convenient surface.[9]

Nineteenth-century images show that, in line with the Royal Order, screens were often given decorative cresting, though in most cases it has subsequently been removed (Fig. 2).[10] The cresting often supported the Royal Arms, and, in cases where there was a tympanum above the screen, there might be one or more of the Ten Commandments, Lord's Prayer and Creed, thus jogging the memory of the many without prayer books. One may speculate that this was also helpful to the more literate youth of the parish when being catechised in church on Sunday afternoon – these were the three texts people needed to know to be permitted to take communion. Surviving examples date from throughout our period.

What of the condition of screens? A survey of churches in West Sussex in 1602 – a rare surviving response from a national survey instigated by Archbishop Whitgift – paints a detailed picture in a poor, rural, and rather conservative region.[11] The inspectors found a range of faults: unwhited walls, unglazed windows, unpaved floors, inadequate pulpits, ramshackle seating, and so on – in other words, exactly as expected in rural churches of this period. But no rood lofts (or Roods) were reported. Of the approximately 150 churches, a little over ten percent (seventeen) had faults with their screen, comments including 'decayed and not at all bewtified', 'unwhited' (implying normally whitewashed at this date), and 'wanteth a payre of dores' (so screen doors were expected, in this diocese at least). But just two were reported as having no partition at all. Another inspection was carried out in 1636, checking compliance with the new Laudian requirements (see below); again, very few churches were reported as not having screens.

It is striking that about 90 percent of the screens which were present at these surveys have since disappeared.[12] Similar high rates of loss have been found elsewhere, and apply to both medieval and new-build screens. Destruction was particularly frequent in the nineteenth century,[13] though unfortunately losses did not stop then: at Compton (Surrey) in about 1994 the seventeenth-century screen – possibly unique in that its decoration matched that of the contemporary altar rails – was deliberately moved out of sight behind a new organ (Fig. 3, and see Fig. 7).

Much of Elizabeth's reign saw a make-do-and-mend approach to church interiors, as reflected in the 1602 survey, but from perhaps the

Fig. 3: St Nicholas, Compton, Surrey, looking west in 1904. This digitally enhanced image shows the upper centre part of the chancel screen, moved to the west end in 1869, and removed in about 1994. The S-shaped carvings match those of the contemporary communion rails. (Photo: Reproduced by permission of Surrey History Centre)

1590s there was an accelerating trend towards refurbishment, centred on urban churches and spilling over to rural areas.[14] In parallel, there was a small but growing number of clergy whose theology led them to emphasise the intrinsic value of the external aspects of worship – music, ceremonial, vestments, the beauty of the church, the presence of imagery – with an emphasis on public prayer and sacramental liturgy rather than preaching. Their opponents nicknamed them 'Arminian', associating them with the controversial Dutch theologian Arminius, and the name stuck (as had the nickname 'puritan'). Arminian influence culminated in the appointment of Richard Neile as Archbishop of York in 1632 and William Laud as Archbishop of Canterbury in 1633. These two archbishops systematically set out to change the setting of parish worship – the so-called Laudian movement, which amongst other things required removing galleries and ensuring uniformity of seating, ideally facing east towards the chancel. More controversially, the table was to be railed in with its long side against the east wall; previously, following initial confusion early in Elizabeth's reign, it was normally in a lengthways orientation, usually in the body of the chancel.[15]

We can see the Laudian engine at work in the 1637 survey of nearly 120 rural parishes in the archdeaconry of Buckingham. Amidst the mass of removing, repairing, replacing and re-ordering to meet the new norms, some 20 churches required improvements to their partition. Usually the concern was not the partition itself, but the removal of 'boards'; although in many cases ambiguous, probably these boards were normally forming a tympanum occupying the top of the arch – as at Iver, where 'the boards on the top of part[itio]n, whereon the

Comm[andmen]ts are written, to be taken down'. This dislike of the tympanum is found elsewhere, and reflected concerns about openness and tidiness, not about the position of the Decalogue. However, in none of these Buckinghamshire churches was the lack of a partition noted.[16]

Overall the data show that a high proportion of churches did indeed keep their screens.[17] Their ubiquity is apparent in the few surviving church plans of the period. For example, a 1636 plan of St Helen's, Worcester (Fig. 4), shows individual stalls, probably the medieval ones, returning against the screen in an arrangement similar to that at Tilney All Saints (Fig. 1). The 1610 sketch plan of the church at Lower Peover (Cheshire; Fig. 5) shows a pre-Laudian arrangement, the table standing lengthways, the dotted line probably at this date indicating the medieval step, though it could be a rail.[18] To the north (left on the plan) is a high-status pew; on the south are stalls of unknown date returning against the screen. The church retains much woodwork of the seventeenth century, and the screen (now gone) may have been of that date judging by the round doorhead shown on the plan. In both plans the nave seating butts right up against the screen, an indication of the pressure on space. Contemporary plans frequently show this, and it may be the

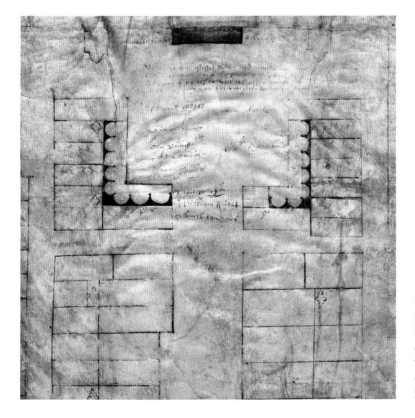

Fig. 4: St Helen's, Worcester: seating plan of 1636, east to the top, detail showing chancel. (Worcestershire Archive and Archaeology Services, f850 Worcester St Andrew; BA: 4426; Parcel: 20; © the PCC of All Saints Worcester)

Fig. 5: St Oswald's, Lower Peover, Cheshire, seating plan of 1636, east to the top, detail showing chancel. (Cheshire Archives and Local Studies P4/8/2)

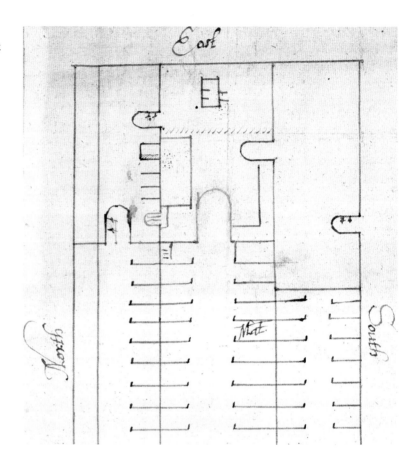

reason that dados often had to be replaced in Victorian times – they had been kicked and bashed over the years, or in the case of new-build screens might perhaps be crudely made in the first place because not exposed to view.

New-build screens

Tilney All Saints is one of approximately 70 extant chancel screens in England thought to have been new-built between 1560 and 1640, approximately one twentieth of the number of medieval screens surviving whole or in part. Very many more have been lost.[19]

Most of the surviving new-build screens have little or no documentary evidence, and it is difficult to answer even the most basic questions. However, fourteen of them do carry dates or precisely datable donors (see Table 1), and this shows that the practice of introducing new screens was alive and well from at least the early 1600s, not surprising in the light of the increasing investment in church furnishings mentioned earlier. This is important to emphasise because, until the Laudian period, early seventeenth-century bishops' and archdeacons' visitation articles show an almost complete disregard for screens – clearly they are not reflecting what was actually happening on the ground.[20]

Decade starting	Number
1600	2
1610	4
1620	4
1630	4
Total	*14*

Table 1: Number of surviving chancel screens bearing dates, by decade.

The dated screens are discussed in the Annex to this chapter, 'A Survey of fourteen dated screens'. Not surprisingly, the Survey suggests that new screens were often introduced as part of a general refurbishment, or when a church was rebuilt. Of the fourteen screens, we know the donors in ten cases: although it was the parish's responsibility to provide a screen (as confirmed in the Royal Order), two of these were paid for by the parish and eight by well-to-do individuals. The very high proportion of individual donors is perhaps surprising: however the small number of screens with dates may be biased towards individual donors, so this ratio may not apply to the many others without dates. We simply do not know.

The very limited evidence does not suggest that those erecting screens before the Laudian period were promoting an Arminian agenda, or held anything other than conventional religious views. Taken as a whole the evidence suggests that putting up a new screen was not a partisan act; it was conformist. There may have been additional local motivations – a chancel screen did, after all, mark the boundary of a space where the rector had particular responsibilities (repair) and rights (including seating and burial) – but they are obscure.

The Survey also suggests that there is nothing to distinguish screens of the Laudian period from others – for example no improvement in quality, and no introduction of overt religious symbolism. One must not assume that a high-quality screen dates from the 1630s. This concurs with much other evidence that well before the Laudian period, middle-of-the-road parishioners and patrons could be willing to spend significant sums of money on church furnishings.[21]

Fig. 6: St Mary the Virgin, Croscombe, Somerset: pulpit of 1616, screen probably of about the same date.

A spectacular example of pre-Laudian furniture of the highest quality is the frequently illustrated ensemble of screen and pulpit at Croscombe (Somerset; Fig. 6); the pulpit is dated 1616, and some similarities in detail suggest that the screen was made at about the same time. It is possible that the designer of both objects was from the circle of William Arnold, the architect-mason who worked at various great houses in the West Country and was responsible for building Wadham College, Oxford (1610–13), including probably designing the chapel screen, and whose home was at Charlton Musgrove, just fifteen miles from Croscombe.[22] Whoever the designer, Croscombe is a reminder that high-end church furniture would have been made by those with secular experience. Furthermore, in terms of design – though not of function – the better-quality screens in parish churches are part of a family which includes domestic screens as well as those in other ecclesiastical settings, such as institutional and private chapels.

In stark contrast to Croscombe, many new-build chancel screens are simple objects, rarely illustrated in books. A good many have turned balusters or simple muntins, often closely spaced, beneath a horizontal beam, often moulded. The beam is supported by substantial wooden pillars, which may be moulded or shaped (Figs 7, 14–16). Church woodwork of this period might be painted, and this would have brought life to the structure.[23] Unlike pre-Reformation screens which sometimes had to support vaulting and a loft, there were no complex structural issues at the junction between vertical element and horizontal beam, so here the joiner had a relatively free hand. Thus small arches are sometimes introduced between the balusters; or there may be tracery at the top of the openings, though this is unusual (Figs 8 & 9). A common alternative is for the screen to be arcaded with relatively wide openings, with a carved semi-circular arch between each vertical element, which itself may be fluted or have fancy capitals – that is to say, standard Jacobean arches, no different from those found on a host of other furnishings. Some examples whose approximate dates are known are collected in Figure 10, and others will be found within the illustrations to the chapter.[24]

As for religious decoration, winged angel faces are occasionally found on chancel screens of our period, but are also found on other types of partition, so are not to be taken as indicating that the chancel is a 'sacred space';[25] probably they were seen as conventional decoration for any church furniture, continuing an earlier tradition. In only one case known to the author is significant religious figurative sculpture found on a new-build screen, at North Newton in Somerset, very much

Fig. 7: St Peter, Farnborough, Hampshire, the seventeenth-century chancel screen (perhaps 1630s), moved to a transept in about 1964, now with cupboards in front. The west-end gallery has identical rectangle-and-oval decoration.

Fig. 8: Ornamenting the tops of balusters. 8a (*left*): St Michael's, Church Stowe, Northamptonshire, one-time chancel screen, now in the south aisle, possibly dating from the building works of 1639. 8b (*right*): St James the Great, Idlicote, Warwickshire. Much altered but retains the alternating miniature Ionic and square-headed capitals supporting a plank decorated with arches and studs.

a one-off (Fig. 10b).[26] A few screens display grotesques or mythological animals similar to those found on secular screens (cover illustration and Figs 11, 19, 21, 22). This willingness to carry overtly secular figural decoration into a church setting is found on other furnishings, and continued a medieval practice which to the modern mind is somewhat puzzling.

On pulpits of the period, scriptural quotations are quite common, the selected texts urging the preacher on,[27] so by analogy, one might have expected on screens to find texts relevant either to those sitting in the nave, or to communicants passing through the screen door. However only two new-build chancel screens are known to the author to carry biblical texts. One of these (Cartmel Priory, Cumbria) is unique in many other ways and not discussed in this chapter, and on the other

Fig. 9: Tracery at the head of chancel screen lights. 9a (*left*): St James the Great, Dauntsey, Wiltshire. The turned balusters (date unknown) support ogee arches separated by trefoils, carved from the solid plank, as in medieval screens. Is this the re-use of medieval material? 9b (*right*): Holy Trinity Church, Barsham, Suffolk. Date of screen unknown; frilly Jacobean tracery, pointless and pretty.

(Geddington, Northamptonshire; Fig. 17) the text appropriately speaks of love of the church building as the House of God. The somewhat anodyne Latin poem on the screen at Abbey Dore is discussed below. A more interesting example is at Baddesley Clinton (Warwickshire; Fig. 25) where a Latin tag hints that something special takes place in the chancel, and it is notable that the patrons and donors of the screens at Geddington and Baddesley Clinton were both from Roman Catholic families (the Treshams and Ferrers respectively).[28]

So neither carvings nor texts were normally used as a means of instruction, or to provide devotional focus, or to signal that beyond the screen lay a sacred space. In fact, most surviving screens are simply acting as a partition, and give little clue as to whether it is a chancel or a private pew and mausoleum that lies beyond. Indeed, some chancels did

Fig. 10: Examples of arcaded lights in chancel screens. 10a (*top left*): St Mary's, Chilton Foliat, Wiltshire, probably of about 1629 when the body of the church was rebuilt by John Packer. 10b (*top right*): St Peter's, North Newton, Somerset, probably of about 1637 when the new church was completed. The screen is exceptionally unusual in having religious figural sculpture ('Hope' with her symbol of an anchor is on the left of the image). 10c (*bottom left*): St Andrew's, West Stafford, Dorset, perhaps of about 1640 when there was significant rebuilding work. 10d (*bottom right*): Kingston Lisle, Oxfordshire, date unknown.

accommodate private pews (e.g. Fig. 5) and many were mausoleums. Placing crosses or Roods above these screens transforms the way we react to them: it is important not to project this back to the early modern period (see e.g. Fig. 24).

An unusual, indeed exceptional, example of a screen indicating what lay beyond was to be found at St Giles-in-the-Fields, London, in the 1630s, a church famous (or infamous) for its highly-developed ceremonial. A communicant entering the chancel (tellingly referred to as the *Sanctum Sanctorum*) passed through:

> a large Screene in the figure of a beautifull Gate, in which is carved two large pillars, and three large statues: on the one side is *Paul* with his sword, on the other, *Barnabas*, with his Booke, and over them *Peter* with his Keyes, they are set above with winged cherubims, and beneath supported by Lions.[29]

This uninhibited Arminian display was easily matched by some of the Cambridge colleges but was extremely unusual for a parish church. Unsurprisingly, with the change of regime, in 1644 the screen at St Giles was taken down. However, to the best of this author's knowledge this was one of only two partitions in a parish church to fall victim to the iconoclasm of the 1640s; the other was at Great St Mary's Cambridge, erected by the ardent Arminian, John Cosin.[30] Notably, the list of church furnishings banned by Parliament did not include screens.[31] Of themselves, they were no longer a matter of active religious controversy.

Two case studies

St John's, Leeds

The distinction between rich display on a screen and Arminian theology (or Laudian requirements) can be teased out at two churches, St John's, Leeds, and All Saints, Wakefield (both in Yorkshire), the subjects of our first case study.

By the 1630s the fast growth of Leeds had led to the parish church becoming severely overcrowded. To relieve this, a local philanthropist, John Harrison, built St John's as a chapel-of-ease. After careful negotiation about future rights and obligations, the chapel (later a parish church) was consecrated on 21 September 1634 by Archbishop Neile.[32]

The vicar in puritan Leeds was chosen by committee, and Harrison himself supported puritan preachers. However, unlike some puritans, he did not seek significant reformation of the national church: he firmly supported episcopacy, the Prayer Book, and the Canons, and disapproved of those puritans who criticised what he called 'trifles' such as the use of the surplice and 'any little ceremony'.[33]

The plan of his church reflects these entirely conventional views. The nave, for preaching, is approximately square, with the screen crossing the church to create a large rectangular chancel. The pulpit with its reading desk was off to one side, more or less in the centre of the north wall (it has since migrated somewhat to the east). Despite this, as far as we know most seats faced east, except for a possible group along the north wall to the east of the pulpit which may have looked west (i.e. facing the preacher).[34] What is certain is that the seat-pricing meant that the well-off sat not at the front of the church as was normal, but towards the north, near the pulpit, with poorer folk towards the south; so there was a psychological north-south axis to the building.

Two communion cups were gifted in 1634, suggesting considerable numbers were expected. The unusually large chancel was probably intended to ensure that despite this there was no need to take communion in pews in the nave as happened at the overcrowded parish church. The chancel had stalls with desks, probably of some quality, on all four sides of the chancel, including the eastern wall: so this was not at all a Laudian arrangement. However, the present table, probably the original, is decorated with small heads on just three of the four sides, with no signs of their having been removed from the eastern side, suggesting it did stand against a wall; it is not known where, nor whether it was railed in.[35]

Overall, the north-south axis to facilitate preaching and the arrangement of the chancel make this a church far removed from Laudian requirements. Nevertheless, the interior is astonishingly rich. Not least the screen is magnificent (front cover), covered in carved foliage and grotesques (but no religious imagery). Interestingly, some contemporary puritans were uneasy: they accused Harrison of the 'popish sin of superstitious merit' and of building his church 'for that end', though their concern may have been the money spent on display rather than the theology of grace embodied in the church services. Harrison felt that such criticism was an 'injurious scandal'.[36]

Stylistic analysis shows that both the wood carving and the decorated plasterwork were the work of craftsmen associated with Francis Gunby, a Leeds man. Gunby and some of his team were expert plasterers and accustomed to carving wooden patterns for plasterwork without any undercutting, which explains why the carving on the screen looks as though it has been applied to the surface although it is in fact carved from the solid.[37] The same team built the screen at All Saints, Wakefield (now the cathedral), which is very similar to that at Leeds, though smaller – indeed, the Wakefield churchwardens probably asked for the Leeds screen to be used as a model (Fig. 11). It has one particularly interesting feature: the lower part of the pre-Reformation screen was kept by Gunby's team and cased in, with a new superstructure above (the original upperwork had probably been removed at an earlier date). Perhaps the presence of pews butting up against the screen made casing-in the easiest solution.[38]

The Wakefield screen was part of a major refurbishment mandated by the authorities. At about the time that St John's was nearing completion, Archbishop Neile was pursuing an anti-puritan programme at major towns in the region, including demanding that church interiors be re-ordered. At puritan Wakefield he took a 'view' (inspected the church): as a result, a new pulpit and screen were introduced, the font was raised and gilded and the seating round it rearranged, and the seating at the east end of the chancel removed. The table was turned altarwise and railed

Fig. 11: All Saints, Wakefield, West Yorkshire, now the Cathedral, showing a detail of the chancel screen of 1634. Despite appearances, the carving is from the solid, not applied to the surface.

in and – most unusually – given a canopy. Two years later, following a further 'view', the nave seating was made uniform. Thus, unlike St John's, this interior explicitly reflected Laudian requirements, though the preaching and (probably) practice remained firmly puritan.[39]

So these two very similar screens could be placed in interiors representing different theologies, one Laudian, one not. This strikes home at Slaidburn church (Lancashire) where there is a very similar screen, probably built between 1633 and 1636.[40] On its own this rich screen does *not* tell us that this was ever a Laudian interior, and with no documentation, and with subsequent changes having disrupted the layout of the church, we can say nothing about the theological opinions of those who placed it here.

Abbey Dore

Our final screen (and second case study) is Abbey Dore in Herefordshire, an enormous parish church occupying the crossing and east end of a Cistercian abbey. The creation of the church from the abbey ruins was funded by Viscount Scudamore, a friend both of Laud and the Arminian Matthew Wren, and himself most definitely an Arminian. How well does the screen (Fig. 12) indicate his religious views?

The church was consecrated on Palm Sunday (22 March) 1635, with a fair measure of clerical choreography. Wren, who had been made Bishop of Hereford a few months before, had some input into the consecration service, though was unable to attend.[41] In the chancel Scudamore had put his theology on display by reinstalling the pre-Reformation high altar of the abbey, a single piece of stone some twelve feet long: it is hard to imagine a more definite statement. Above it he introduced stained glass depicting the Ascension, and behind this a carved altar piece, now lost, whose subject is not known. Inside the chancel were both the minister's pew and reading desk; the people sat on the other side of the screen, in the nave, which occupied the transept. The pulpit was also in the nave. Scudamore's views are apparent in all aspects of the planning of the interior.

Scudamore said that 'Churches should be magnificall & great'. The screen is indeed 'magnificall'; if it were painted – and traces of blue paint are said to have been found – its appearance would lighten considerably, especially as the rather heavy dado would have been hidden by seating, Scudamore's pews going right up to the screen.[42]

The carpenter and master builder John Abel was contracted to build the new roofs and the woodwork of the belfry. The screen too is probably his. Not only does it match the general style of his work, still to

Fig. 12 : Dore Abbey, in the village of Abbey Dore, Herefordshire, showing the screen (completed by March 1635). The photograph is taken from the south transept.

be seen in the one-time market hall of Leominster (now Grange Court) completed by him and his team in 1634, but there are two particular design features (bunches of grapes and lettering) which are found on the external walls at Grange Court and both on the screen and in the roof at Abbey Dore.[43]

Unusually, there is an inscription on the screen. This is in the form of a memorable (because short and rhyming) and perhaps well-known Latin poem.[44] There is nothing deeply religious about the poem – it is a general invocation to the reader to be grateful to God, to avoid wrongdoing, and to be dead to this world and ready for the next. It is telling that Abel or his clients felt that it was also an appropriate choice for the outside of Leominster town hall, where it can still be seen.

It would seem, then, that this screen – taken on its own – is, like the others, silent about its donor's theological views. Except that, as communicants left the chancel, they walked under a carving of the Five Wounds of Christ (Fig. 13), an image whose close association with Roman Catholic piety makes it literally shocking to find in an English parish church of this period.[45]

Fig. 13: Dore Abbey, the pediment above the east side of the screen door, with a carving of the Five Wounds of Christ.

Summary

In summary, although Roods and rood lofts disappeared following the accession of Elizabeth, rood screens did not; the great losses occurred in subsequent centuries. Thus pre-Reformation rood screens were ubiquitous, providing the 'comely partition' between the chancel and the nave required by Elizabeth's 1561 Order.

Some new screens were built from at least the early seventeenth century: putting up a new chancel screen was not an extreme act, or making a point – it was conformist. Although new screens followed the medieval design of a panelled base below an open arcade supporting a top beam, they vary in both quality and detail of design, with no chronological development, though individual designers or carpenters could create screens with a family resemblance. A high-quality screen did not necessarily represent Arminian sympathies, and those built during the Laudian period are normally indistinguishable from those built previously.

The newly-built screens of our period very rarely carry texts. The occasional representation of winged angel faces is probably merely conventional, and any other figural carving is usually secular. Thus for the most part these new screens do nothing explicit to instruct, to evoke devotion, or to suggest that the chancel to which they lead is a holy or sacred space.

In many, perhaps most, cases it may have been enough for parishioners, donors and the church authorities that the new screen was both 'comely' and a 'partition'.

ANNEX: A survey of fourteen dated screens

This Survey discusses the fourteen chancel screens of our period which bear dates (or have dateable donors). The first ten predate 1630.

North Baddesley, Hampshire, 1602

The earliest dated chancel screen, simple but well-constructed, is at North Baddesley church in Hampshire, north of Southampton (Fig. 14). It bears the date 1602 and the initials 'TF', for Sir Thomas Fleming, an MP and leading London lawyer. It may have come from the church at nearby North Stoneham, where Sir Thomas was also patron and had a fine manor house. So this, the earliest dated screen, was commissioned by a wealthy, well-connected and urbane gentleman. Perhaps he was responding to the 1602 survey, discussed earlier; or perhaps this was the rural equivalent of contemporary moves to improve the City of London churches.[46]

Harthill, Cheshire, 1609

The screen at Harthill, Cheshire was made for the new church, built in 1609, and tells a rather different story.

The top beam is carved with egg and dart, so originally it was probably a neat piece of work; but it was badly mangled in 1863, and today is in a sorry state (Fig. 15). Along the beam the inscription records that 'This church was builded upon the devoc'on of the cuntrye by

Fig. 14: St John the Baptist, North Baddesley, Hampshire, facing north-east, showing the screen dated 1602.

Fig. 15: All Saints, Harthill, Cheshire, facing north-east, a detail of the screen of 1609. The inscription is original, the coats of arms Victorian. (Photo: Cameron Newham)

the labor and travell [travail] of Ed Tanat Io [John] Dod Tho Bulckley & Ra[lph] Weston P[?arson] Ao 1609'. This might suggest a demotic building campaign, but three of these four people were local gentry and the fourth was the vicar. So here in a diocese far removed from London and its ways, the minister and his gentry supporters provided a partition as a routine part of fitting out a new church.[47]

Vowchurch, Herefordshire, 1613

The church at Vowchurch, Herefordshire was given a new roof in 1613 (based on a carved coat of arms on one of the timbers). From the style, the carpenter was probably John Abel, a name encountered at Abbey Dore.

The screen is probably also of 1613 (Fig. 16), as this date and a short Latin motto associated elsewhere with Abel are amateurishly inscribed on a plaque which used to hang above the screen. The screen's heavy design is slightly offset by the figures either side of the door, and a panel with carved sea monsters above (assuming these are original to the screen): the monsters are similar to, though cruder than, those on

Fig. 16: St Bartholomew's, Vowchurch, Herefordshire, facing east. The screen is probably of 1613.

Abel's town hall of Leominster (now Grange Court, Leominster). The male and female figures resemble those on contemporary fireplaces and door frames, an impression heightened by the pediment above which has (not visible in the photograph) a flower vase lightly incised, itself a common Renaissance motif.[48]

Another plaque, more carefully cut, explains that 'Heare Below ly The body of Thomas hill ande Marget his Wife Whose Children Made This Skryne'. Unfortunately nothing is known about the Hill family,[49] nor whether 'made' means 'constructed' or 'donated'. This unselfconscious use of vernacular carpentry by a (presumably) local family is the opposite of a polite, urban refurbishment, and a reminder that much church furniture in this period was probably of poor quality (cf. Fig. 25), a fact easy to overlook as it is the best which tends to survive.

Geddington, Northamptonshire, 1618

The splendid screen at Geddington, Northamptonshire, now in the south aisle (Fig. 17), is of unique design, having an arched top which fitted into the medieval chancel arch, mimicking the tracery of the

Fig. 17: St Mary Magdalene, Geddington, Northamptonshire, the chancel screen, now at the entrance to the south aisle chapel, from the west. The screen is dated 1618.

fourteenth-century east window. The screen's donor was Maurice Tresham from the neighbouring village of Newton, a member of an important local Catholic family; its design includes the 'Tresham trefoil'. Round the edge of the screen runs Psalm 26:8 ('Lord, I have loved the beautie of thine house and the place where thine honour dwelleth', a translation from the Vulgate), and over its doorway is 'quid retribuam domino' ('What can I give to the Lord?'). Why Tresham gave the screen, and what stimulated the design is unknown, though its looking back to gothic forms may hint at an affection for the old ways.[50]

Tilney All Saints, Norfolk, 1618
This screen is discussed in the introduction to this chapter (Fig. 1).

Fig. 18: St Peter and St Paul, Kedington, Suffolk, looking east. The screen, here shown wide open, is dated 1619. The Barnardiston pew to the left is made up from the medieval screen.

Kedington, Suffolk, 1619

The screen at Kedington, Suffolk, dated 1619 was installed under the aegis of the influential puritan Sir Nathaniel Barnardiston; the medieval screen was used to make his squire's pew (Fig. 18). Uniquely among survivors, the screen subverts its purpose by having three folding doors, thus ensuring the church can be opened into a single space. This suggests that the puritan Barnardiston[51] – an influential man, far removed from Arminianism – disliked fixed screens. But he still included a form of partition in his parish church. Why? – to mark out the boundary between the parish's and rector's territory? because it was 'normal'? for some other reason? We do not know.

Bruton, Somerset, 1620

Quite different is the high-quality screen at Bruton (Somerset; Fig. 19). According to the inscription, this was introduced in 1620 by John Sampson and 'H. I.' (Hugh Ivye), churchwardens together for the year ending April 1620; Sampson (but not Ivye) continued in the role a further two years.[52] The screen is currently at the west end entrance and much altered, but the general view is that it was originally the chancel screen, placed under the tower when the chancel was rebuilt in 1743, and later moved to the west entrance.[53] The church was re-seated and re-roofed in the first part of the seventeenth century, so perhaps the screen was introduced as part of a wider programme. It includes medieval work in the dado, as at Wakefield (discussed above). Otherwise it has the feel of a domestic screen: the carved imagery is unapologetically secular, including, for example, a cloven-hoofed piper.

Fig. 19: St Mary the Virgin, Bruton, Somerset. Looking north-west, detail of screen dated 1620, now at the west entrance. The door by the wall is a later insertion.

Empshott, Hampshire, 1624

At the tiny church of Empshott, in Hampshire, the narrow chancel screen is now at the west entrance (Fig. 20). As the inscription explains, this was given by James Metcalfe in 1624. His will shows he was a very wealthy yeoman farmer who had died the previous year, leaving the not overly generous sum of thirty shillings to the church.[54] The donation of the screen was probably part of a larger refurbishment project: the font cover is dated 1626, and the communion rail, the pulpit, some seating, the now-removed east window and (probably) the wooden tower are all of about this date.[55]

Although it is notoriously difficult to establish an individual's religious views from the preamble to a will, Metcalfe's does give a hint. It is unusually long and includes an extended quotation from 'A Prayer for a Sick Man, when He is Told that He is not a Man for this World, but must Prepare Himself to Go unto God', from the best-selling *Practice of Piety* by Lewis Bayly.[56] Metcalfe's appeal to his Maker is heartfelt and can still move the modern reader, but the theology (our particular concern) is centrist and conventional.

Fig. 20: Holy Rood, Empshott, Hampshire. Detail of chancel screen dated 1624 now in the porch, seen from the west. Note the surviving colour.

Metcalfe's will directed that James Rowlandson, from the neighbouring parish, should preach at his funeral service. Rowlandson was one of the Southampton town preachers, and probably a capable man in the pulpit. His patronage by Bishop Bilson and his chaplaincy to Charles I suggest that he was no puritan, though his three published sermons are not noticeably Arminian.[57]

One of these sermons was preached in 1620 when Bishop Andrewes, a leading Arminian, consecrated the new chapel of ease at Peartree, Southampton (though he had no hand in choosing Rowlandson as preacher). A more junior Matthew Wren (see Abbey Dore, above) was also in attendance. The church had a chancel screen (now lost), but more striking is the communion vessel, purchased with money collected at the consecration, which is in the form of a pre-Reformation chalice, the earliest example in a parish church of a distinctive style which became associated with Arminianism.[58] This is a straw in the wind, but may indicate the direction in which the diocese of Winchester was being taken at this relatively early date.[59]

So Metcalfe, the donor of the screen, was unlikely to have been a puritan and may have been aware of emerging Arminian thinking. Perhaps more pertinently, he was probably responding to the very specific needs of his own parish church.

Washfield, Devon, 1624

Of the same date, 1624, but a complete contrast, is the screen at Washfield (Devon; Fig. 21). This is a fine object, almost a medieval screen in classical clothes, with Corinthian columns and a cornice carved with foliage, beasts and grotesques. It is surmounted by the Royal Arms, with the Prince of Wales feathers over that part of the screen in front of the north chapel, which belonged to the Worth family, patrons of the living.[60]

The plaque on the screen is dated 1624, with the name Bernard Seridge, placed over a 'W' with a tilde. The rector, Edward Seridge, had a son called Bernard, and this is probably our man.[61] The 'W' might signify that Bernard was warden (sadly, the churchwardens' accounts are damaged for this period).[62] Or perhaps it indicates that the Worth family contributed to the screen, part of which separated off their chapel. Or maybe it stands for 'Washfield'. The possibilities are not quite endless.

Edward Seridge, the rector, was licensed by Bishop William Cotton to preach throughout the diocese, so would not have been a radical. In addition to Washfield, he was also rector of nearby Calverleigh, a living which he resigned in September 1624 at the age of about 54.[63]

Fig. 21: St Mary the Virgin, Washfield, Devon, facing east, showing the screen dated 1624.

The following March, being 'sick of body', he made his will, desiring to be buried in the porch of Washfield church 'there to remain till the day of Resurrection', and a month later he died. His will does not mention the church, but at some stage he paid for the refurbishing of the chancel at Calverleigh, so one might speculate that he also gifted the money for the Washfield screen, put up by Bernard his son.[64]

Whoever the donor of this fine screen, we know nothing of the motive for its introduction. Was it diocesan pressure? Local pride in the church? Personal display? Its entirely secular carvings do rather rule out it being an aid to devotion, a means of instruction, or a reminder to communicants of the nature of the Eucharist; but in the absence of contemporary commentary there is a limit to how much can be gleaned from church furnishings alone.

Rodney Stoke, Somerset, 1625

Our final screen of the pre-Laudian period is at Rodney Stoke in Somerset, dated 1625 and bearing the initials of Sir Edward Rodney, who presumably donated it (Fig. 22). The communion table is dated

Fig. 22: St Leonard's, Rodney Stoke, Somerset, detail of upperwork of the screen which is dated 1625.

1634, and the communion rails, font cover and pulpit look to be of a broadly similar date, whilst certain repairs to the fabric can be tentatively dated to no earlier than 1628, all suggesting the screen was part of a wider re-ordering, one perhaps covering a decade or more. The devotional notes written for his children suggest that Sir Edward was a conscientious and thoughtful Protestant, but no Arminian. The need to maintain and upgrade his church in keeping with his station may have provided sufficient motivation for the screen, particularly as his family mausoleum lay in the north chapel.[65]

As at Washfield, this reminds one of a medieval screen, albeit with Renaissance dress. Heightening this impression is a balustraded parapet, where it is said a music gallery once stood. At the restoration in 1879 the screen was left alone, apart from reducing the height of the door by eighteen inches, 'as otherwise the officiating clergyman would have been almost concealed from the congregation.'[66]

Four screens of the mid 1630s

The last four screens date from the Laudian period, and will be taken together. They are at Thurloxton (Somerset), Warnford (Hampshire), and Baddesley Clinton (Warwickshire) all dated 1634; and Stonegrave

(North Yorkshire) dated 1637. All except Baddesley Clinton were in dioceses with Laudian bishops, but no general conclusions can be drawn from that: the sample is too small and the policy of individual bishops regarding screens not well enough understood.

The screen at Thurloxton (Fig. 23) records the names of the churchwardens who put it up in 1634 (since painted over with later names). It is a handsome piece. In the eighteenth century it was painted green with red roses, and this colour scheme may perhaps have been original.[67] Little is known of Warnford (Fig. 24): the rector of this estate church was a Laudian (and future Archbishop of York), but he was an absentee, and may have played little part in decisions about the furnishing of his church. In 1958 the dado was lowered as it was 'partly obscuring the view of the chancel and altar', and arcades were introduced above the balusters. There is food for thought here (and at Rodney Stoke, above), about churchgoers' expectations of sightlines in the seventeenth century, as they sat in their high pews.[68]

Fig. 23: St Giles's, Thurloxton, Somerset, facing east, showing the screen of 1634 (since altered) and the pulpit with its unusual figures (cf. Fig. 10b for a similar figure). The lectern is not original to the screen.

Fig. 24: Parish church of Warnford, Hampshire (unknown dedication), facing east. The screen is dated 1624. The dado was lowered in 1958 when arcades were introduced. The hanging rood is by Martin Travers, 1938.

Baddesley Clinton is another estate church (which often preserve older internal arrangements through conservatism or poverty). In 1634 the chancel was completely rebuilt and the screen inserted by Edward Ferrers, the owner of the big house (Fig. 25). It is a crude piece of work; but money was short. Ferrers was a loyal Catholic, though he attended the parish church, and it may not be coincidence that one of the three

Fig. 25: St Michael's, Baddesley Clinton, Warwickshire, the screen (dated 1634) from the west.

Latin tags on the screen can be translated as 'away from here, go away, impious ones', which could be interpreted as indicating that sacred space lay beyond; whilst those who knew their Virgil might also have recognised the allusion to a place of sacrifice.[69]

The screen at Stonegrave (Fig. 26) has northern and southern sections which form flat-headed canopies. No one knows why: possibly they emphasised the place of the reading desk and clerk's desk. A nineteenth-century illustration and the remnants of a brutal Victorian restoration suggest that new chancel furnishings may have been introduced at about the same time as the screen.[70] The rector here was a puritan: possibly he and his parish were pushed into a chancel refurbishment as part of Archbishop Neile's Laudian programme.

Nothing about these four screens shouts 'Laudian' to the observer. They vary as much in their design and quality of construction as those made in previous decades, and cannot be distinguished from them.

Fig. 26: Holy Trinity (Stonegrave Minster), Stonegrave, North Yorkshire, the screen (dated 1637) from the east. (© petelovespurple, CC BY-NC-SA 2.0)

Appendix:
Extract from the Royal Order of 10 October 1561

Imprimis, for the avoiding of much strife and contention that hath heretofore risen among the Queen's subjects in divers parts of the realm, for the using or transposing of the rood-lofts, fonts, and steps within the choirs and chancels in every parish church, It is thus decreed and ordained, that the rood-lofts, as yet, being at this day aforesaid untransposed, shall be so altered that the upper part of the same, with the soller, be quite taken down unto the upper parts of the vaults, and beam running in length over the said vaults, by putting some convenient crest upon the said beam towards the church, with leaving the situation of the seats as well in the choir as in the church as heretofore hath been used.

Provided yet, that where any parish, of their own costs and charges by [?common] consent, will pull down the whole frame, and re-edifying again the same in joiner's work (as in divers churches within the city of London doth appear), that they may do as they think agreeable, so it be to the height of the upper beam aforesaid.

Provided also, that where in any parish church the said rood-lofts be already transposed, so that there remain a comely partition betwixt the chancel and the church, that no alteration be otherwise attempted in them, but be suffered in quiet. And where no partition is standing, there to be one appointed.[71]

Notes

1. This chapter looks only at screens in parish churches, not those in other ecclesiastical settings. It develops my earlier work in Trevor Cooper, 'The Interior Planning of the English Parish Church, 1559–*c*.1640', in Paul Barnwell and Trevor Cooper (eds.), *Places of Worship in Britain and Ireland, 1550–1689*, Rewley House Studies in the Historic Environment 10 (Donington, 2019), 52–94 (pp. 56–60, 80). Previous surveys of screens of this period include Frederick Bligh Bond and Bede Camm, *Roodscreens and Roodlofts* (1909), vol. 1, section 4; Aymer Vallance, *English Church Screens* (1936), chap. 10. Photographs are mine unless stated otherwise. I am grateful to Michael Bundock, Andrew Foster, Richard Halsey, Mark Kirby, Susan Orlik and Robert Walker for comments on an earlier draft.
2. For communion practice, Trevor Cooper, *The Puritan Chancel Arrangements at St Mary's, Deerhurst and their Context* (Deerhurst, forthcoming).
3. E. Whitaker, *Martin Bucer and the Book of Common Prayer*, Alcuin Club Collections 55 (Great Wakering, 1974), 14–16; E. Hunt, *The Life and Times of John Hooper* (Lewiston, 1992), 47–74, 161–5, 277–83; John Hooper, *Early Writings of John Hooper*, ed. Samuel Carr, (Cambridge, 1843), 492.

4. Trevor Cooper, 'Planning', 56.

5. See e.g. Eamon Duffy, *The Stripping of the Altars: Traditional Religion in England c.1400–c.1580* (1992), 568–9; Ronald Hutton, 'The Local Impact of the Tudor Reformations', in Christopher Haigh (ed.), *The English Reformation Revised*, (Cambridge, 1987), 115–38, (pp. 134–5); Patrick Collinson, *Archbishop Grindal 1519–1583* (1979), 118; Ronald Hutton, *The Rise and Fall of Merry England*, repr. (Oxford & New York, 1996), 108–9.

6. Hutton, 'Impact', 135–6; Duffy, *Stripping*, 570–77; Margaret Aston, *Broken Idols of the English Reformation* (Cambridge, 2016), 164–83.

7. Cooper, 'Planning', 60–66, 73–5.

8. Lucy Wrapson, 'East Anglian Medieval Church Screens: A Brief Guide to Their Physical History', *Hamilton Kerr Institute, Bulletin*, no. 4 (2013), 33–47, (pp. 40, 41, 45 n41); H. Harrison and J. West, 'West Country Rood Screens: Construction and Practice', in Spike Bucklow et al (eds.), *The Art and Science of the Church Screen in Medieval Europe: Making, Meaning, Preserving* (Woodbridge, 2017), 135; David Griffith, 'Texts and Detexting on Late Medieval English Church Screens', ibid., 71–99, (pp. 96–9).

9. For example, Attleborough and Binham Priory (both Norfolk), Lydeard St Lawrence (Devon) and (if not Victorian work) Elworthy (Somerset).

10. For discussion of Folke (Fig. 2c), Susan Orlik, 'The "Beauty of Holiness" Revisited: An Analysis of Investment in Parish Church Interiors in Dorset, Somerset and Wiltshire, 1560–1640' (PhD, Birmingham, 2018), 68, 96–9.

11. Joan Barham and Andrew Foster, *Church Surveys of Chichester Archdeaconry 1602, 1610 & 1636*, Sussex Record Society, vol. 98 (Lewes, 2018). I am grateful to Dr Foster for stimulating discussion of this and other matters.

12. Survivors from Elizabeth Williamson et al., *The Buildings of England: Sussex: West* (2019); churches entirely rebuilt were not counted.

13. Cooper, 'Planning', 58; Wrapson, 'East Anglian Screens', 42.

14. Cooper, 'Planning', 80–83; Barham and Foster, *Surveys*, xxx.

15. Kenneth Fincham and Nicholas Tyacke, *Altars Restored: The Changing Face of English Religious Worship, 1547-c.1700* (Oxford, 2007), esp. chap. 5.

16. R. Gibbs, 'The State of the Buckinghamshire Parish Churches in the 16th and 17th Centuries', *Records of Buckinghamshire* 6 (1887), 150–67, 245–58, (Iver, p. 165). For 'boards' in the city of Cambridge, William Palmer (ed.), *Episcopal Visitation Returns for Cambridgeshire* (Cambridge, 1930), 29–39. For northern examples, Ronald Marchant, *The Puritans and the Church Courts in the Diocese of York, 1560–1642* (1960), 63. General discussion in Fincham and Tyacke, *Altars Restored*, 242–3.

17. Cooper, 'Planning', 56–60.

18. Previously reproduced in George Yule, 'James VI and I: Furnishing the Churches in His Two Kingdoms', in Anthony Fletcher and Peter Roberts (eds.), *Religion, Culture, and Society in Early Modern Britain: Essays in Honour of Patrick Collinson*, (Cambridge, 1994), 182–208 (p. 198). For context, Walter Horn and Ernest Born, 'Two Timbered Mediaeval Churches of Cheshire: St. James and St. Paul at Marton and St. Oswald at Lower Peover', *The Art Bulletin* 44, no. 4 (December 1962), 263–78 (p. 271).

19. Based on Michael Good, *Compendium of Pevsner Buildings of England*,

2nd ed. (CD, Yale, 2005) and subsequent research. I have visited more than forty of the seventy, and almost as many tower and parclose screens.

20. Cooper, 'Planning', 80 for brief discussion.

21. Cooper, 'Planning', 80–85; Orlik, 'Beauty of Holiness', passim; Margaret Bullett, 'Post-Reformation Preaching in the Pennines: Space, Identity and Affectivity' (PhD, Huddersfield, 2016), passim.

22. I hope to discuss Croscombe at a future date.

23. Harrison and West, 'West Country Rood Screens', 131–35. Examples of painted screens in: M. Ramsay and Alison Maddock (eds.), *The Churchwardens' Accounts of Walton-on-the-Hill, Lancashire 1627–1667*, Record Society of Lancashire and Cheshire, 141 (2005), 29; Thomas Steel, *Prescot Churchwardens' Accounts, 1635–1663*, ibid., 137 (2002), 9–10.

24. Supporting references for Fig. 10 captions as follows. Fig. 10a: Stephen Porter, 'John Packer', *Oxford Dictionary of National Biography* (henceforth ODNB) (2008); Fig. 10b: Orlik, 'Beauty of Holiness', 142; Fig. 10c: inscription on south wall of church.

25. For example, the parclose screen at Pluckley, Kent (1635) and tower screen at Odell, Bedfordshire (1637).

26. Orlik, 'Beauty of Holiness' 138–42.

27. Orlik, 'Beauty of Holiness', 165.

28. See relevant entries in the Annex. The Latin tags on the remnants of the new-build screen at Ringsfield, Suffolk (where the Arminian author, Robert Shelford was minister 1599–1639) were, I believe, painted relatively recently.

29. *The Petition and Articles Exhibited in Parliament against Dr Heywood . . .* (1641), 5.

30. But not Cosin's screen at Brancepeth, Co. Durham (Trevor Cooper, 'Seventeenth-Century Twin Pulpits in England', *Ecclesiology Today*, no. 55 & 56 (2017), 7–46 (pp. 26–9)).

31. Trevor Cooper (ed.), *The Journal of William Dowsing: Iconoclasm in East Anglia During the English Civil War* (Woodbridge, 2001), 47–55, 156–89, 196–203; Julie Spraggon, *Puritan Iconoclasm During the English Civil War* (Woodbridge, 2003), 154–5, 257–61.

32. John Ellis Stocks, 'The Church of St. John the Evangelist, New Briggate, Leeds: Chiefly Concerning the Woodwork and Carving', *Thoresby Society Miscellanea* 24, part 2 (1916), 190–226; Janet Douglas and Ken Powell, *St John's Church Leeds: A History* (1982); Kimberley David Murray, 'Puritanism and Civic Life in York, Newcastle, Hull, Beverley and Leeds' (PhD, Durham, 1990), 354ff (negotiations); J. Wickham Legg, *English Orders for Consecrating Churches*, Henry Bradshaw Society 41, (1911), 192–8, 358 (consecration). The story that Robert Todd the puritan preacher at the consecration was immediately suspended is probably not true (Ronald Marchant, *The Puritans and the Church Courts in the Diocese of York, 1560–1642* (1960), 116–17).

33. Maggie Bullett, '"Son of Thunder or Good Shepherd", Contesting the Parish Pulpit in Early Seventeenth-Century Leeds', *Northern History* 55, no. 2 (2018), 161–77; T. Whitaker, *Loidis and Elmete* (Leeds, 1816), appendix (separately paginated) 10–12 (in which, see esp. 'saying' no. 3).

34. Stocks, 'St. John', Fig. 1; Bullett, 'Son of Thunder', 40.

35. Marchant, *Puritans*, 116; Stocks, 'St. John', Fig. 3, 211, Fig. 21; 'Three Churches in Leeds', *The Ecclesiologist* 8, no. 63 (December 1847), 134; J. Sprittles, *A Survey of the Plate of Leeds Parish Church and Its Ancient Chapelries*, Thoresby Society Monographs 2 (Leeds, 1951), 22–5, plate VI. Laura Bonnington and Clare Chapman of the Churches Conservation Trust kindly inspected the table's east side.

36. *Loidis*, appendix 14 ('extempore prayer').

37. David Bostwick, 'Decorative Plasterwork of the Yorkshire Region, 1570–1670' (PhD, Sheffield, 1993), 32, 64, 127–8, 133–4, 137.

38. John Walker, *The History of the Old Parish Church of All Saints, Wakefield* (Wakefield, 1888), 113–14 incl. plate, 154–5. The screen has been heavily restored.

39. Andrew Foster, 'Church Policies of the 1630s', in Richard Cust and Ann Hughes (eds.), *Conflict in Early Stuart England: Studies in Religion and Politics 1603–1642* (Harlow, 1989), 193–223, (pp. 204–7); Marchant, *Puritans*, 107–22; Walker, *All Saints*, 112–15, 127, 269; Bullett, 'Son of Thunder', 150.

40. James Mawdesley and Christopher Spencer, 'The Politics of the Chancel Screen: Samuel Moore, Slaidburn, and the Parochial Dynamics of Laudianism', *The Seventeenth Century* 29, no. 4 (2014), 359–80, (pp. 363, 367–8).

41. Ian Atherton, 'Viscount Scudamore's "Laudianism": The Religious Practices of the First Viscount Scudamore', *Historical Journal* 34, no. 3 (1991), 567–96; Jim Tonkin, 'The Scudamore Restoration', in Ron Shoesmith and Ruth Richardson (eds.), *A Definitive History of Dore Abbey*, (Little Logaston, 1997), 163–72. Jim Tonkin, '"Beauty of Holiness": The East Window', in ibid., 185–94; Matthew Gibson, *A View of the Ancient and Present State of the Churches of Door, Home-Lacy and Hempsted* (1727), 38. Wren's liturgical practices derived from Lancelot Andrewes' private chapel (Peter McCullough, 'Absent Presence: Lancelot Andrewes and 1662', in Stephen Platten and Christopher Woods (eds.), *Comfortable Words: Polity and Piety and the Book of Common Prayer* (2012), 49–68). Abbey Dore shows little or no indication of being based on Andrewes' chapel (*pace* Ruth Richardson, 'The 17th Century Abbey – as Lord Scudamore Knew It', *Dore Abbey Newsletter*, Dore Article 34 (2010)). Wickham Legg, *Orders*, pp. lvi, 146–91, 353–8 (for Wren, 354).

42. Atherton, 'Laudianism', 586. Ruth Richardson, 'Colour in Dore Abbey', *Dore Abbey Newsletter*, Dore Article 35 (2010). Shoesmith and Richardson, *Definitive History*, frontis; ICBS 1898 plan at http://images.lambethpalacelibrary.org.uk.

43. Edwin Sledmere, *Abbey Dore, Herefordshire, Its Building and Restoration* (Hereford, 1914), 71; D. Gregory, *John Abel of Sarnesfield, Carpenter*, Caradoc and Severn Valley Field Club Occasional Papers 5 (1980), 7–11; D. Whitehead, 'John Abel', *ODNB* (2004). I am grateful to Robert Walker for a tele-photograph of the church roof.

44. *Vive deo gratus / toti mundo tumulatus / crimine mundatus / semper transire paratus*. The poem, known from a variety of sources, was perhaps

popularised by the many editions of Henry Greenwood, *A Treatise on the Great and Generall Daye of Judgement . . .* (1st edn 1606) (for which see Ian Green, *Print and Protestantism in Early Modern England* (Oxford, 2000), 624).

45. Abel may have been a Roman Catholic (Gregory, *John Abel*, 4).

46. J. Baker, 'Sir Thomas Fleming', *ODNB* (2008). 'North Baddesley', and 'North Stoneham' in William Page (ed.), *A History of the County of Hampshire: Volume 3* (1908), 463–5, 478–81; Cooper, 'Planning', 82–3.

47. Raymond Richards, *Old Cheshire Churches* (1947), 180–84; Godfrey Mathews, 'Notes on the Parish and Church of Harthill', *Transactions of the Historical Society of Lancashire and Cheshire* 81 (1929), 38–50 (pp. 40–44); Fred Crossley, 'The Church Screens of Cheshire', ibid. 69 (1917), 1–63 (pp. 59–60). For Dodd and Tannatt, J. Rylands and F. Beazley, 'The Monuments at Bunbury Church, Cheshire (Part 2)', ibid. 70 (1918), 72–130, (pp. 116–17); for Thomas Bulkley [sic] at Bickerton, *Memorials of the Duttons of Dutton in Cheshire* (1901), 221; for all three, John Rylands (ed.), *The Visitation of Cheshire in the Year 1580*, Harleian Society 18 (1882) and George Ormerod, *The History of the County Palatine and City of Chester* (1819), vol. 2, 359, 369, 390–92. For Weston, 'Clergy of the Church of England Database 1540–1835' at https://theclergydatabase.org.uk/ (henceforth CCED): clergy id 23988 (for Malpas, of which Harthill was a chapel of ease), 23989 and 34315 (for Harthill) (possibly identical clerics of the same name; see also ids 121737, 34313).

48. George Marshall, 'Some Account of the Churches of Vowchurch, Turnastone, St Margaret's Urishay and Peterchurch', *Transactions of the Woolhope Naturalists' Field Club* (1916), 93–195, (p. 95); pre-1840 watercolour in church. Gregory, *John Abel*, 5. I am grateful to Richard Halsey for helpful discussion on this and Washfield screen.

49. Ex info Steve Edwards, churchwarden.

50. Christopher Markham, *The History and Antiquities of Geddington, Northamptonshire* (Northampton, 1899), 19. I am grateful to Kam Caddell for various discussions.

51. R. Greaves, 'Sir Nathaniel Barnardiston', *ODNB* (2008).

52. D. Hayward (ed.), *The Registers of Bruton, Co. Somerset* (Parish Register Society, n.d.), 7–18.

53. R. Carpenter, 'Parish Church of Bruton', *Proceedings of the Somersetshire Archaeological and Natural History Society* (henceforth *SANHS*) 24, no. 1 (1878), 32–7 (p. 36); A. Baggs and M. Siraut, 'Bruton', in C. Currie and R. Dunning (eds), *A History of the County of Somerset: Volume 7* (1999), 18–42; Phyllis Couzens, *Bruton in Selwood*, revised edn. (Sherborne, 1972), 25, 29–30.

54. The National Archives (TNA) PROB 11/142/545.

55. *Church of the Holy Rood, Empshott, Liss, Hampshire,* 2nd edn (1999).

56. First published 1612 (Green, *Print and Protestantism*, 348–51).

57. I am grateful to Andrew Thomson for help with Rowlandson (*c*.1577–1639), for whom: CCED (clergy id 15181); Anthony Wood and Philip Bliss, *Athenae Oxonienses*, new edition (Oxford, 1848), vol. 2, 637; Joseph Foster, *Alumni Oxonienses*, Early Series (Oxford, 1891), vol. 3, 1286; TNA PROB 11/180 (will).

58. Charles Oman, *English Church Plate 1597–1830* (Oxford, 1957), 205–6, 313–14; P. Braithwaite, *Church Plate of Hampshire* (1909), 309–10. Wickham Legg, *Orders,* 47–80 (esp. pp.50, 67), 338.

59. Surviving church court papers are unlikely to be helpful on this (based on Peter Abraham, '"For a Decent Order in the Church": Ceremony, Culture and Conformity in an Early Stuart Diocese, with Particular Reference to the See of Winchester' (PhD, Hull, 2002)).

60. J. Turner, *Washfield: The Story of a Devonshire Village* (Tiverton, 1947), 18–21.

61. Devon Archives, Oswyn Murray, *Abstracts of Wills*, vol. 29.

62. Devon Archives, 1146A/add/PW/1. See also S. Madge, 'Church-Wardens Accounts of Washfield Parish, Devon, 1561–1903, Analysed' (1948), British Library (BL) 10351.i.28, fol. 128.

63. CCED two ids: 101522, 102531; Murray, *Abstracts*; S. Madge, 'Records of Washfield Parish' (1948), BL 010368.y.11, vol. 1 fol. 143, vol. 3 fol. 76.

64. George Oliver, *Ecclesiastical Antiquities of Devon*, ?2nd edn., vol. 1 (Exeter, 1840), 99, 101.

65. Cooper, 'Planning', p.59n24. I am grateful for Dr Orlik's help with Sir Rodney.

66. 'Rodney Stoke', *SANHS* 34 (1888), 30; *The Western Daily Press, Bristol,* Friday, 15 August 1879, 5.

67. Mark McDermott and Sue Berry (eds.), *Edmund Rack's Survey of Somerset* (Padstow, 2011), 237; R. Grosvenor Bartelot, 'St Giles' Church Thurloxton' (copy in church September 2013), (1911); Orlik, 'Beauty of Holiness', 138–43.

68. CCED id 12760. Leaflet, 'The Church of our Lady, Warnford', n.d.

69. Henry Norris, *Baddesley Clinton* (1897), 54, 73, 76–78; Elizabeth Berry, *Henry Ferrers an Early Warwickshire Antiquary*, Dugdale Society Occasional Papers 16 (Oxford, 1965), 4, 17–18. The inscription reads: *Memor esto brevis aevi : hie querite regna Dei : procul hinc, procul este prophani* (the latter from Virgil, *Aeneid*, VI, line 257).

70. W. Eastmead, *Historia Rievallensis . . .* (1824), 187; Rosalind Field and Dav Smith, 'Afterword: Robert Thornton Country', in Susanna Fein and Michael Johnston (eds.), *Robert Thornton and His Books: Essays on the Lincoln and London Thornton Manuscripts* (York, 2014), 267–72; Elanor Pitt, 'Not All Those Who Wander Are Lost: Reconstructing the Post-Medieval Phase of Stonegrave Minster Using a Buildings Archaeology Approach' (MA, York, 2019), Fig. 142 and passim; Marchant, *Puritans*, 257.

71. Walter Frere and William Kennedy (eds.), *Visitation Articles and Injunctions of the Period of the Reformation*, 3 vols., Alcuin Club Collections, XIV, XV, XVI (1910), vol. 3 (i.e. XVI) 108–9.

Chapter 4

A Patristic Experiment: The Screens of Sir Christopher Wren's Churches

MARK KIRBY

After the Restoration of the monarchy in 1660, there was a two year hiatus before any new chancel screens were erected. In that period, the Church of England gradually reasserted itself, cementing its own re-establishment in the Act of Uniformity of 1662. Bishops and archdeacons re-established the system of visitations, and the old system of appointment of clergy to parochial livings by patrons resumed quickly. Humphrey Henchman, Bishop of Salisbury wrote:

> In church government I find no such discouragement but that I hope
> … I shall regulate the clergy of the diocese in the same manner as they
> were governed twenty-four years since.[1]

In the same year as the Act of Uniformity, we find what may be the earliest chancel screen erected after the Restoration – at St Saviour's, Foremark in Derbyshire (Figs 1 & 2). Built next to his house by the local squire, Sir Francis Burdett, the fabric of the church is in seventeenth-century gothic, expressing the conviction that gothic is the language of church architecture. Inside, the furnishings also look back to pre-War stability, but only as far the earlier part of the same century. The pews are fairly work-a-day but the pulpit and screen are finely executed in Jacobean style. The screen is quite inventive. Its structure resembles a domestic screen as much as a church one, with not a single liturgical message expressed in wood. Only the glass panel in the rather amateurish pediment – showing the Holy Spirit and two angels – gives that expression.

Possibly, like the choice of gothic architecture, it too expresses a conviction that a chancel *should* have a screen – given added poignancy by being installed so early after the Restoration. It is very charming, but is essentially a continuation of the phenomenon of post-Reformation screens from before the Civil War.

Fig. 1: St Saviour's, Foremark, Derbyshire (unknown architect, 1662). Built in seventeenth-century perpendicular style for the local squire, Sir Francis Burdett, St Saviour's effectively ignores the political effects of the Civil War and Interregnum, and aligns itself with an earlier age. (Photo: Mark Kirby, 2019)

Fig. 2: St Saviour's, Foremark, interior view facing east. The chancel screen is a fine piece of craftsmanship, though lacking ecclesiastical references. (Photo: Mark Kirby, 2019)

This chapter considers two screens of a different character, erected in two parish churches newly built in the City of London by Sir Christopher Wren after the Great Fire of 1666. These were installed at St Peter Cornhill in 1680–81 and at All Hallows-the-Great, probably in 1683 (Figs 3 & 4).[2]

In these two parishes, we see the agency of two clergymen at work, though most likely with the support of their vestries and wider parishioners. Immediately, one very obvious observation to make is that only two churches installed such screens, out of the total of 51 churches built in this period, whether in the Fire-damaged City or further west. Their extreme rarity therefore makes them interesting as an indication

SOUTH VIEW OF THE CHURCH OF St PETER upon Cornhill, LONDON.

London Published 1 January 1812 by Robert Wilkinson, N°125 Fenchurch Street.

Fig. 3: St Peter Cornhill, London (Sir Christopher Wren, 1677–81). A view of 1825 engraved by Thomas Dale after a drawing by John Whichelo, from Robert Wilkinson's *Londina Illustrata* (1834).

Fig. 4: All Hallows-the-Great, Thames Street, London (Sir Christopher Wren, c.1677–81/82). The cramped settings of many of the new churches meant that Wren expended little on external form or decoration. A view of 1814 engraved by John Coney after a drawing by Joseph Skelton, from John Booth's *The Architectural Series of London Churches* (1814).

ALL HALLOWS the GREAT.
United with
ALL HALLOWS the LESS.

of a particular point of view of the two rectors concerned, as well as probably being unrepresentative of the clergy and vestrymen of the City at large. Nevertheless, the motivation which led those two clergymen to decide that a screen was not just desirable but necessary was the same as that of all parishes in addressing their own furnishings in general. It was to express their notions of ecclesial identity visually inside their churches.

Even if it was a waning tradition, we might have expected more than two of the Wren churches to have been given screens. Absent any contemporary comment, we need to consider why there weren't. One possibility is that, while screens had not been sufficiently odious to the

Parliamentary authorities to provoke their demolition, nor did they have a clear purpose anymore. Thus, it was not obvious that a screen destroyed in the Fire needed to be rebuilt afterwards. Additionally, Wren did not build any of the new churches with a physically distinct chancel of medieval proportions – that is to say, one large enough for choir stalls as well as places for the clergy.[3] Consequently, a screen placed across the opening of the small chancel spaces at St Edmund-the-King for example – only sixteen feet, six inches wide – would look odd, enclosing on the fourth side what was already a very small space (Fig. 5).[4] It is, more accurately, a railed sanctuary rather than a chancel.

Likewise, in the churches which Wren built with a rectangular, basilican, or a central plan, the architecture of the building did not provide a distinct chancel-like space across which one might place a screen. And any screen, therefore, would have had to run the full width of the church in order to create that space, which is precisely what the screens at St Peter Cornhill and All Hallows-the-Great do. If, then, Wren eschewed physically distinct chancels in the architectural design of the churches, and if there was a prevailing view across the City as a whole that screens were no longer necessary in their furnishings, why were they installed at St Peter Cornhill and All Hallows-the-Great at all?

Fig. 5: St Edmund-the-King, Lombard Street, London (Sir Christopher Wren, 1670–74), the 'chancel' and reredos. A screen erected across such a small space would have been nonsensical.
(Photo: Mark Kirby, 2014)

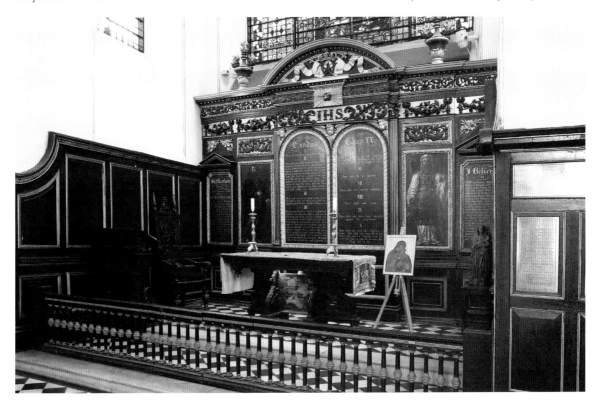

St Peter Cornhill

The Cornhill screen was the first of the two to be installed, in 1680 (Fig. 6). This came approximately half-way through the period during which the City churches were being built and furnished, or, to put it another way, after half of the churches had already been built and furnished without a screen. By that stage, there was a well-established pattern of vestrymen visiting each other's new churches and ordering their craftsmen to copy the pulpit at one, or the gallery front from another, the font at a third, and so on. When it came to screens, however, the master joiners at St Peter's had nothing to go on.

The Cornhill screen is closer to the new classical style than those at Croscombe and Leeds discussed in the previous chapter by Trevor Cooper, and it omits the mannerist pinnacles, obelisks, and strapwork decoration characteristic of that earlier period. These would have been thoroughly old-fashioned by Restoration standards, and it would be interesting to know if the joiners or the parish contemplated the use of a contemporary alternative – urns or acroters for example. The joiners paid due regard to the fabric of the church, and the columns of the centre arch are copies of the pilasters of the east wall behind

Fig. 6: St Peter Cornhill, interior view facing east, showing the pulpit, screen and reredos beyond. The east windows are by C. A. Gibbs, 1872. The church is currently in use as a study centre.
(Photo: Mark Kirby, 2015)

Fig. 7: St Peter Cornhill, detail of the centre of the screen, showing the double-hanging-arch motif, cavetto cornice and the Royal Arms. (Photo: Mark Kirby, 2015)

them. The upward sweep of the cavetto cornice at the centre creates a nice theatrical space for the Royal Arms, which are set in a cartouche over the centre arch and flanked by a lion and a unicorn standing on pedestals. It is a pleasant and more three-dimensional alternative to the usual wall-mounted arrangement, executed in relief.

The arcades to either side, however, are struggling with the grammar of classical architecture. They retain a double-hanging-arch motif which is also present at Croscombe and other early seventeenth-century locations, and which is more a feature of Jacobean style than Restoration (Fig. 7). In contrast to surviving medieval screens, the lack of a need for a vault to support a roodloft frees the design to become even more delicate. But this comes at a price. The proportions of the arcade columns show that the joiners were aware of the rules of the classical orders. They have tried to compensate for the extreme narrowness of the columns by increasing the height of the plinth to about one quarter of the whole arcade height, indicated by the addition of a notional plinth-cap half-way up. This leaves the top half roughly in the correct proportion of width to height. Arguably, the fragility of the arcades is no different to that of many medieval screens, and it conveys the same lightness of touch as some East Anglian screens do. It was, after all, never the purpose of such screens to block the view to the chancel, but rather to signal the significance of its separation from the nave and, as we shall see in this case, to facilitate the notion of congregational movement from one space to another.[5] However, the classical rules of proportion and the orders make it more difficult to achieve the delicacy at which perpendicular gothic tracery so excels.

Fig. 8: All Hallows-the-Great, interior view, c.1890. This image illustrates the way in which the furnishings of the Wren churches were conceived as an integrated whole. (Courtesy of the LAMAS Glass Slide Collection, Bishopsgate Institute, London: Slide C140)

Fig. 9: All Hallows-the-Great, detail of the screen, now installed at St Margaret Lothbury, London, showing the fretwork pilasters at the centre of the screen and the double-helix colonettes. The painting of Aaron, and its corresponding painting of Moses off to the left, were originally at St Christopher-le-Stocks. (Photo: Mark Kirby, 2014)

The screen at All Hallows-the-Great followed that at Cornhill two years later (Fig. 8). All Hallows was demolished in phases up to 1894 and the screen was transferred to St Margaret Lothbury. It has the same delicacy as that at Cornhill and has other features in common: the double-hanging-arch motif, slender columns – here in the form of double spirals – and a cavetto cornice, sweeping up at the centre. The double-spiral columns cleverly avoid the problem of faithfulness to the orders by omitting any form of classical treatment altogether. The arrangement of the centre is different: the delicacy of the double spiral columns of the arcade is matched by a pierced, or fretwork pair of flat pillars supporting an open compass pediment (Fig. 9).

Within the break of the pediment sits a florid set of Royal Arms, and below its cornice, an eagle is suspended with its wings open and ribbons billowing to either side. This eagle is unique in Wren's churches and has given rise to a myth that the screen was given by the Hanseatic League, whose London base – the Steelyard – was in the parish.[6] This has been disproved and, in any case, the Hanseatic eagle was double-headed, and one might have expected the Hansa merchants to have depicted their own emblem correctly.[7] It is more likely that the eagle represented the gospel, in the same way that countless brass eagle-lecterns do across the country. It also responds to the smaller eagle set on the front of the sounding board a few feet away. Perhaps placing a symbol of the gospel on the screen roughly in the position of the unacceptable medieval Rood also helped to detoxify any remaining suspicion that screens were inherently Catholic in nature.

Understanding the two rectors involved here is the key to understanding what these screens are about. The seventeenth-century Church of England was unusually preoccupied with the study of patristics – the writings of the Early Church Fathers – variously defined as the period up to the conversion of the Emperor Constantine, or as late as 600AD. It was a preoccupation which sometimes baffled continental observers, but at its core was the desire to demonstrate that the Church of England was directly descended from the Early Church, when theology and the worship of God could be characterised as having been at their purest. The Church of England had therefore preserved that purity by leaving a Roman Church, which had corrupted and distorted it.

The two rectors were William Beveridge (who became bishop of St Asaph in 1704) and William Cave. Both were noted patristics scholars who wished to express their belief in the patristic pedigree of the Church of England not only in their writings but also in the furnishings of their respective parish churches. Fortunately, we have two sources which provide rich information on their thinking about the purpose of screens in churches, especially Beveridge's. The first source is Beveridge's 1672 treatise on the Councils and Canons of the Early Church, *Synodikon* – specifically a chapter which describes the layout and use of primitive church buildings.[8]

The second source is an influential sermon which Beveridge preached at the opening of his church in 1682, which was published in at least 39 editions under the title *The Excellency and Usefulness of the Common Prayer*.[9] In *Excellency*, Beveridge draws a parallel between Early Church practice and contemporary Anglican practice in various areas, in particular between the 'Skreen or Partition of Network' in primitive churches and the chancel screen of later ones.[10] His comment about the screen is brief and made in a section which is principally an intense exposition of the spiritual importance of the Lord's Supper. Beveridge marks this out as 'the highest Ordinance of the Church,' requiring 'the highest pitch of Devotion that we can arrive at in this world.' Indeed, 'nothing contributes more than frequent Communion at our Lords Table' to ensuring that Christians 'might be edified and confirmed in the Faith.'[11] Anxious not to delay his main eucharistic theme for too long, Beveridge adds as an aside:

Some perhaps may wonder why [a chancel screen] should be observed in our Church, rather than in all the other Churches which have been lately built in this City. Whereas they should rather wonder why it was not observed in all other as well as this. For besides our Obligations to conform as much as may be to the practice of the Universal Church, and to avoid novelty and singularity in all things relating to the Worship of God; it cannot be easily imagined that the Catholick Church in all Ages and places for 13 or 1400 years together, should observe such a Custom as this, except there were great reasons for it.[12]

The screen was clearly no mere antiquarian whimsy on Beveridge's part. He felt obliged to install a screen, and his disapproval of churches without them should be taken at face-value. However, his reference to primitive practice as the justification for installing a screen is problematic. This becomes clearer when we compare the lengthy description of an Early Church building in *Synodikon* (Fig. 10) with what he actually installed at Cornhill.

In *Synodikon* Beveridge identifies no fewer than nine different spiritual classes of person present, each of whom is assigned to a particular role and place. These begin with the 'wailers' – those with the lowest spiritual status – who stand in the portico seeking to demonstrate their sincerity to those who are allowed to enter further.[13] Three further classes of penitent stand in the narthex, where they may, in separate groups, first 'learn,' and then 'hear' what is happening inside the church building.[14] Inside the church itself, Beveridge describes further separations of laity into three groups, also determined by their spiritual state. Finally, the bishop and his deacons occupy the sanctuary at the eastern part of the church.[15] At each stage, Beveridge relates these classes to the architectural features of the church, paying particular attention to the believer's progression from the portico, through to standing east of the lectern, in front of the sanctuary screen.

Beveridge did not write *Synodikon* specifically with Cornhill in mind, and his descriptions focus as much on Early Church spirituality and liturgical practice as they do on architectural features. These unsurprisingly highlight the difference between those primitive practices and seventeenth-century Anglican practice. For example, a faithful person caught swearing was forced back into the position of a wailer, taking another nine years to get back to being one of the faithful again. More notably, the ancient exclusion of so many laity from communion contrasts powerfully with the legal requirement of Canon 21 that all English men and women receive communion three times per year.[16]

This is a conundrum, and we need to conclude that the screen in St Peter Cornhill must be read as an evocation and allusion to something of particular ecclesial and theological importance. Nevertheless,

Fig. 10: Conjectural groundplan of an early Christian church, from William Beveridge's *Synodikon* (1672), II, plate opposite 71. The plan shows the importance of multiple, segregated spaces in early Church architecture.

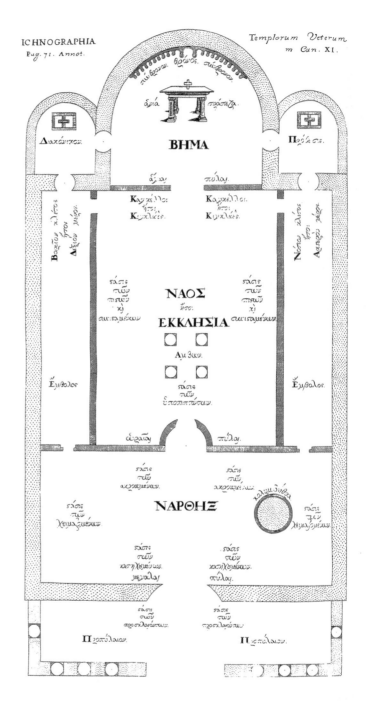

it is an evocation in the loosest possible sense. Beveridge was not concerned with a precise archaeological reconstruction of Early Church architecture or its internal layout. In one sense, this did not matter. The source inspiration was that the Church of England was the heir of antiquity. It therefore required that there be a screen, and Beveridge

 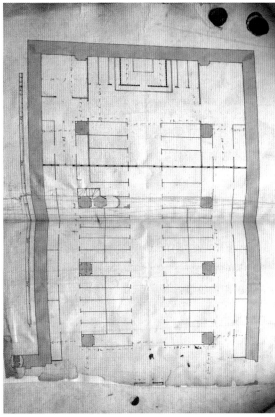

Fig. 11 (*left*): St Peter Cornhill. An interior view of 1825 engraved by Thomas Dale after a drawing by John Whichelo, from Robert Wilkinson's *Londina Illustrata* (1834). The engraving clearly shows the way in which the screen signifies the 'otherness' of what lies beyond.

Fig. 12 (*right*): St Peter Cornhill. Pew plan by the joiners Messrs Poultney and Athew, attached to their contract with the parish, 1680. LMA/P69/PET1/B/001/MS04165/001, fols. 489–492. (Photo: Mark Kirby, 2014)

provided one. It was enough that he declared it to be an allusion to Early Church practice in order to fulfil its purpose, without needing to appear like something one might find in fourth-century Byzantium.

We see a more overtly seventeenth-century eucharistic purpose for the screen in Beveridge's sermon, *Excellency*. In particular, it is helpful if we read the relevant sections alongside the pew plan drawn up by the joiners and an illustration of the church interior as it first appeared (Figs 11 & 12).

First, the Cornhill screen, and the space behind it, are clearly distinguished from those of medieval origin in the absence of any steps rising to the chancel. Such an ascent had been a key feature of the ideal chancel in the mind of the Laudian party during their brief period of hegemony before the Civil War. More importantly, the screen is placed two bays down the length of the rectangular-planned, basilican church, and it had three rows of pews placed to the east of it. This was a feature to which Laudians had objected strongly.[17] Still more objectionable to Laudians, there are pews set with their ends against the east wall, either side of the communion table and orientated towards it. The Cornhill table did, however, stand on one step and was railed on three sides.

The details of the contract with the joiners tell us that the pews east of the screen were to be made one inch higher than those west of the screen. It is a small detail but, by applying the seventeenth-century rules of decorum, it indicates some notion of difference in status, function, or, in a church context, spiritual significance. In a further illustration from *Excellency* of the attention to liturgical detail which Beveridge brought to the church furnishings, the dimensions of these pews have been specified so as to accommodate kneeling:

> To take off all those little excuses that men are apt to make for themselves in this case, the Seats in this Church are so disposed, and all things so prepared in them, that there can be no inconvenience at all in it, but rather all the conveniences for kneeling that can be desired.[18]

At a height of three feet and nine inches, these pews were shorter than many others in the City churches – those at the neighbouring St Michael Cornhill were five feet tall – and enabled those sitting in them to see the minister at the communion table even when kneeling.[19]

Beveridge describes the key liturgical actions of communion. First, he says that a church chancel has always been understood to be like the Holy of Holies in the Temple of Jerusalem and that it should be kept separate, for use solely for the purposes of communion, and for the congregation to move into that space so that they 'meet together, as one body, in one place separated for that purpose.' He goes on to say that all communicants should all be able to see the consecration of the elements 'and contemplate upon their Blessed Saviour, there evidently set forth as Crucified for them.'

The clear message is that worshippers are seated for most of the service in their allocated pews west of the screen, but move east of the screen for communion, so that they can personally see and hear the blessing of the bread and wine. The implication is that the eastern pews were empty, other than at a communion service, and there is no suggestion that some parishioners were already routinely there. From the number of those eastern pews, we can deduce that administration must have been carried out in groups until all communicants had received. Beveridge emphasises that the Lord's Supper is both a 'Communion with Christ' and a communion 'with one another', and he clearly decided that that mutual communion would be better expressed by enabling a larger number of communicants to gather together, than would be the case if they only met together around the communion rails, which might only have accommodated eight to ten people.[20]

It might be argued against this interpretation that reserving so much space for occasional use would put pressure on seating elsewhere in the church. However, St Peter's is a large church and may have had seats to spare. Moreover, it was a parish which had not been united with another after the Great Fire – as more than half of the parishes were under the terms of the Additional Act of 1670.[21] It therefore did not have the additional pressure of seating the population of two parishes in one building. Lastly, Beveridge attached great importance to communion, saying that his preference would be to hold communion services every week, doubtless justifying reserving an area for that special purpose.[22]

What Beveridge set out at St Peter Cornhill was his own particular approach to providing a space which was dedicated to the Lord's Supper, which provided audibility and visibility for large numbers of communicants, and which made a statement about Anglican descent from the Early Church.

All Hallows-the-Great

Turning to All Hallows-the-Great – which was furnished after Cornhill – William Cave matched Beveridge's patristic efforts with his own screen. Although he did not write specifically about his London church, or publish a sermon which set out his ecclesial thinking in the way that Beveridge did, his own writings, especially *Primitive Christianity*, show that his motivations were the same as Beveridge's in their patristic origins.[23]

Cave was similarly pro-active in taking the furnishing of his church under his own control. Having not attended vestry meetings for quite a while, Cave turned up in June 1683, and the parish clerk underlined his name twice with evident irony. Precisely how Cave intended the space east of the screen to be used routinely is less clear: there were five rows of pews east of the screen – compared with three at Cornhill – and the overall seating capacity of the church was less than at Cornhill.

The building of All Hallows also served two parishes – those of All Hallows-the-Great and All Hallows-the-Less – making it more likely that the eastern pews were routinely occupied, and not just at

Fig. 13: All Hallows-the-Great, the stone reredos, c.1890. It was the only one of its kind in the new City churches. The statues of Moses and Aaron survive at St Michael Paternoster Royal. (Courtesy of the LAMAS Glass Slide Collection, Bishopsgate Institute, London: Slide C141)

communion times. Overall, it therefore seems less likely that Cave was able to set aside his chancel solely for communion in quite the same manner, and his primary interest was the allusion to primitive practice. Possibly, in view of his churchmanship and the exceptional fittings of his reredos (Fig. 13, made of stone and accompanied by statues of Moses and Aaron and a kneeling, bare-breasted woman in marble holding up a stone *mensa*), Cave sought to make an assertion of the special holiness of the sanctuary through the reredos and altar-table rather than by separation of spaces, albeit in a chancel which was compromised by the presence of so many pews.

The models for administering communion described here and in the previous chapter, and the diversity of churchmanship of those involved, serve to emphasise the manner in which differences between the specifics of any individual's eucharistic theology should not mask the fact that all Protestants viewed communion as being sacramentally and spiritually significant, to be undertaken with spiritual care and preparation.[24]

As these brief summaries make clear, for some clergy, it was important that their practical and architectural arrangements reflected their sense that the Lord's Supper was a communion, a shared, participatory action and expression of faith in which, at the Prayer Book invitation to draw near with faith, communicants physically rose from one place and moved to another. There, parishioners gathered together in large numbers in a place in which they could see and hear together all that happened in the communion service. It is this spiritual experience which Beveridge wanted to achieve at Cornhill, to use a screen to mark out, not a Laudian sanctuary made holy by the presence of an altar, but a communion space specially reserved for the corporate celebration, witnessing and sharing of the Lord's Supper.

The other City churches

Given that it was only at two of the new City churches where screens were erected, did the other parish clergy not share Beveridge's and Cave's sense of identification with the Early Church? The attention given to questions of Church identity in the period was intense, and the focus on idealised notions of the Jerusalem Temple and primitive practice was common. Beveridge and Cave stood apart from their London colleagues in being patristic scholars, and it ought not to be surprising that they engaged with the idea of recreating this particular aspect of primitive practice more enthusiastically than others did. However, it is possible that others may have done so too, albeit in a much smaller way, and which was more representational in nature than architectural.

Scholars of the period all commented on the *cancelli*, the rails or screens which existed in early churches. These are variously described as 'Skreen or Partition of Network' (Beveridge), 'neat rails' (Cave), 'open work' and 'fenced in by a Low Wenscot' (Wheler), and 'certain Rails of Wood; curiously and artificially wrought in the Form of Net-work' (Bingham).[25]

Something matching these descriptions – but less substantial than a chancel screen – did indeed exist in many of the new churches. Pews were arranged in blocks, sometimes with a cross aisle and sometimes not. In some cases, at the back of each pew-block stood a 'screen,' twelve to eighteen inches high, carved and usually pierced with acanthus scrollwork or other foliate decoration, as at St Stephen Walbrook (Fig. 14).

Fig. 14: St Stephen Walbrook, Walbrook, London (Sir Christopher Wren, 1672–80). Interior view of 1839, facing east, showing the low screens erected at the rear of each of the four pew-blocks. Engraved by Frederick McKenzie after a drawing by T. Challis, from George Godwin's *The Churches of London* (1839).

Fig. 15: St Mary Abchurch, Abchurch Lane, London (Sir Christopher Wren, 1681–86). The original box pews have been cut down but retain the very finely-carved low screens in several places. More than any other of the surviving Wren churches, St Mary Abchurch still conveys something of its original character. (Photo: Mark Kirby, 2014)

With the nineteenth-century removal of box pews, some of these survived as decoration on other features, and only at St Mary Abchurch is it still possible to see them in something close to their original use and position (Fig. 15). Possibly, when applied in the new churches, these low screens were more than just decorative, but were intended to be a symbolic reference to the *cancelli* of primitive churches.

There appears to be no contemporary reference to support this suggestion, but one person who thought so was the Victorian antiquary the Revd W. Sparrow Simpson. Sparrow Simpson was rector of the Wren church of St Matthew Friday Street, and Vice-President of the St Paul's Ecclesiological Society, and it is possible that he may have been projecting backwards his own churchmanship. Nevertheless, he noted of his own church that:

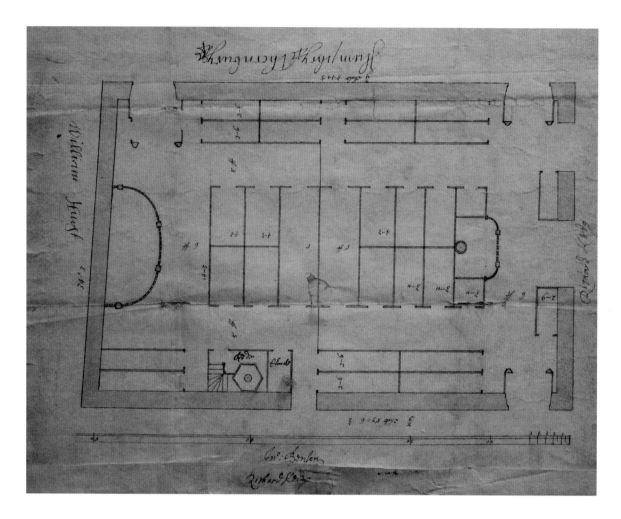

Fig. 16: St Matthew Friday Street,
London (Sir Christopher Wren,
1682–85). 1684 pew plan appended
to contract with the joiner, Richard
Kedge. A pencil line is drawn across
the church separating the front
three pews from those behind
in a notional 'chancel'. LMA/P69/
MTW/B/013/MS07683.
(Photo: Mark Kirby, 2015)

A small carved screen standing upon the pews, scarcely more than 18 inches above the moulding on the backs, divided the church into two parts, forming, as is the case in most of Sir Christopher Wren's churches, a quasi-chancel. This screen was removed but a few years ago, though before my incumbency. From its carved panels, which were fortunately preserved, I have constructed the present reading-desk.[26]

No illustration survives, but the 1684 pew plan appended to the contract with the joiner Richard Kedge shows a line drawn across the church, north-south, dividing three pews east of that line from the rest (Fig. 16).[27]

The same feature can also be seen in three other pew plans for Wren churches.[28] These lines are not directly explained in the parish records. However, the contract for one of these (All Hallows, Lombard Street) also refers to setting up 'pewes in the said Church and in the

Drawn by R.W.Billings.　　　　　　　　Engraved by J.

ST BARTHOLOMEW'S,
By the Bank.

Chancell thereof.'[29] There are also references in the records of four other churches which also had no physically distinct chancel to pews being 'in the chancel': St Antholin, St Lawrence Jewry, St Mary Abchurch, and St Mary Aldermanbury.[30]

Seemingly in Simpson's mind, these low screens did convey meaning, and although he mentions a 'quasi-chancel', he clearly did not have a medieval, or architectural, meaning of 'chancel' in mind. In fact, it is not clear what Simpson meant at all. But additional evidence from St Stephen Walbrook also suggests that these screens were intended to signify in some sense. In the contract for building the pews, the joiners were instructed to make some of the benches for the pews out of oak and others out of the cheaper wood, deal.[31] This suggests that the status of some of those pews, most likely the ones closest to the pulpit, might be reflected in the material of which they are made, as well as by the use of these low screens to demarcate the eastern and western halves.

They are also visible in several other engravings showing the interiors of churches, such as St Bartholomew-by-the-Exchange (Fig. 17),

Fig. 17: St Bartholomew-by-the-Exchange, Bartholomew Lane, London (Sir Christopher Wren, 1675–83). Interior view of 1837 engraved by Robert Billings after a drawing by John le Keux, from George Godwin's *The Churches of London* (1837).

where the status of certain pews seems to be represented by differences in height – three different heights in this case – as well as separation of the eastern-most block by screens. Maybe we see here in a more modest form than at St Peter Cornhill and All Hallows-the-Great, an oblique reference to Early Church practice.

Conclusion

In conclusion, the two screens we have looked at here, though fascinating, were not influential in and of themselves. The eighteenth century went on to be a relatively screen-free century.[32] They were, however, important as part of an on-going pattern of the Church of England seeking to express in its liturgical furnishings the assertion that she was descended from the Early Church – an assertion made in the face of both Roman and nonconformist challenge. The Church of England had identified itself with the Early Church from the start of the Reformation and continued to do so in the eighteenth century. More often, however, these patristic references were made through the central placing of pulpits – or the iconography of the reredos – than they were in the erection of chancel screens.

Notes

1. Public Record Office, S.P. 29/43, fol. 68, quoted in Robert Bosher, *The Making of the Restoration Settlement: The Influence of the Laudians 1649–1662*, (New York, 1951), 236.

2. London Metropolitan Archives ('LMA') P69/PET1/B/001/MS04165/001, fols. 489–492, 504; LMA/P69/ALH7/B/001/MS00819/001, fols. 318, 328.

3. When choir stalls were installed in Wren's churches in Victorian re-orderings, they were all placed in what had previously been the space of the easternmost pews of the nave.

4. Arthur T. Bolton and H. Duncan Hendry (eds.), *The Wren Society,* 20 vols, (Oxford, 1924–43), IX, Plates XXI and XXIII.

5. Eamon Duffy, *The Stripping of the Altars*, (New Haven and London, 2005), 112, 'The [pre-Reformation] screen itself was both a barrier and no barrier. It was not a wall but rather a set of windows, a frame for liturgical drama.'

6. Paul Jeffrey, 'The Great Screen of All Hallows-the-Great,' *Transactions of the Ancient Monuments Society*, 37 (1993): 157–158.

7. Ibid.

8. 'Annotations on the Canons of the First Nicene Council – On Canon XI,' in William Beveridge, *Synodikon sive pandectae Canonum SS. Apostolurm, et Conciliorum ab Ecclesia Graeca receptorum*, (1672), 71–77. I am grateful to David Wyatt for translating this chapter from Beveridge's Latin and Greek text.

9. William Beveridge, *A Sermon Concerning the Excellency and Usefulness of the Common Prayer*, (1682). British Library, *Short Title Catalogue*, online edition, lists 39 editions from 1682 to 1799, including one in Welsh.

10. Pierre de la Ruffinière du Prey, *Hawksmoor's London Churches: Architecture and Theology*, (Chicago, 2000), 31–6; Robin Griffith-Jones, '"An Enrichment of Cherubims": Christopher Wren's Refurbishment of the Temple Church,' in Robin Griffith-Jones and David Park (eds.), *The Temple Church in London: History, Architecture, Art*, (Woodbridge, 2010), 159–163; Peter Doll, *'After the Primitive Christians': The Eighteenth-Century Anglican Eucharist in its Architectural Setting* (Cambridge, 1997), 27; and Peter Doll, 'The Architectural Expression of Primitive Christianity: William Beveridge and the Temple of Solomon,' *Reformation & Renaissance Review: Journal of the Society for Reformation Studies*, 13, no. 2 (August 2011): 275–306.

11. Beveridge, *Excellency*, 25–7.

12. Ibid., 26.

13. Beveridge, *Synodikon*, II.

14. Ibid., VII-VIII.

15. Ibid., XIII.

16. Gerald Bray (ed.), *The Anglican Canons 1529–1947*, (Woodbridge, 1998), 291, 293; Beveridge, *Synodikon*, III, IV, VIII, where all but the Faithfull and 'those standing with them' are commanded to leave.

17. Kenneth Fincham and Nicholas Tyacke, *Altars Restored: The Changing Face of English Religious Worship, 1547–c.1700*, (Oxford, 2007), 132, 143, 187–191, *et passim*.

18. Beveridge, *Excellency*, 29.

19. LMA/P69/MIC2/B/001/MS04072/001/002, fol. 268v.

20. Ibid.

21. *Statutes of the Realm*, edited by John Raithby, 7 vols, (1819–20), 'An Additionall, Act for the rebuilding of the Citty of London, uniteing of Parishes and rebuilding of the Cathedrall and Parochiall Churches within the said City, 1670.'

22. Beveridge, *Excellency*, 28.

23. William Cave, *Primitive Christianity: or, the Religion of the Ancient Christians in the First Ages of the Gospel in two volumes*, (1673), 138–140.

24. For discussion of the importance attached to communion across the theological spectrum, including the implications of receiving the elements worthily or unworthily, see Arnold Hunt, 'The Lord's Supper in Early Modern England,' *Past and Present* 161 (1998): 39–83; and Alec Ryrie, 'The Lord's Supper,' in Alec Ryrie, *Being Protestant in Reformation Britain* (Oxford, 2013), 336–351.

25. Beveridge, *Excellency*, 26; Cave, *Primitive Christianity*, 139; George Wheler, *An Account of the Churches and Places of Assembly of the Primitive Christians.* (London, 1689), 70, 117; Joseph Bingham, *Origines Ecclesiasticae, or Antiquities of the Christian Church*, (1708), 163.

26. W. Sparrow Simpson, 'Notes on the History and Antiquities of the United Parishes of S. Matthew Friday Street and S. Peter Cheap in the City of London,' *Transactions of the London & Middlesex Archaeological Society*, III (1870): 378.

27. LMA/P69/MTW/B/013/MS07683, n.p., dated 11 November 1684.

28. LMA/P69/ALH4/B/001/MS04049/002, fol. 48r.; LMA/P69/STE2/B/025/MS07695.

29. LMA/P69/ALH4/B/001/MS04049/002, fol. 48r.

30. LMA/P69/ANL/B/004/MS01046/001, fol. 289r.; LMA/P69/LAW1/B/001/MS02590/002, fol. 127.; LMA/ P69/LAW2/B/020/MS03925, fol. 6; LMA/P69/MRY2/B/001/MS03570/002, fol. 148v.; LMA/P69/MTW/B/005/MS01016/002, n.p., 28 March 1687.

31. LMA/P69/STE2/B/026/MS01056, fol. 20.

32. There are interesting examples at Holy Sepulchre, Warminghurst (1724) and St Peter's, Parham (*c.*1800), both in West Sussex, and a more eccentric example at St Margaret's, Thorpe Market in Norfolk (1796).

Chapter 5

'A chancel without a screen is scarcely a chancel at all'[1]: The Oxford Movement, A.W. N. Pugin, Camdenians, Ritualists, Evangelicals, and the Rood Screen

JOHN ROBERTS

In the early decades of the nineteenth century, rood screens, or chancel screens of any description, were at best irrelevant in Anglican churches. The 600 new churches built under the terms of the Church Building Acts of 1818 and 1824, whether gothic or classical in style, were almost always designed with the characteristics of the prevailing 'Auditory' church – with the focus on preaching from the pulpit and audibility as priorities.[2] Many new churches had no chancel at all, just an altar table placed in a niche in some notional version of a ritual east end. There were no new rood screens.

Similarly, in the existing stock of medieval parish churches, where many screens had survived, their continued existence had become more a matter of accident than design. Growing interest in medieval features among antiquaries could in rare local cases secure the preservation of a screen, but in general, clergymen, churchwardens and parishioners showed rood screens little or no interest. The need was first to secure the fabric of the church against further decay, as cheaply as possible, and second, in many cases, to increase the total number of places available for growing congregations. This was coupled to a widespread drive to increase the proportion of free, unappropriated 'sittings'. Such improvements were often made at the expense of the chancel. And they could be facilitated by the removal of a decrepit and unwanted screen which took up valuable space in a prime position across the chancel entrance. An illustration of the prevailing style of worship in *The Illustrated London News* of September 1852 shows the elderly Duke of Wellington at worship shortly before his death (Fig. 1). He occupies the large manorial pew at St Mary's, Walmer (Kent), and faces an enormous triple-decker pulpit arrangement, itself in front of what appear to be sash windows with some rather fine drawing room curtains. The entire

Fig. 1: The Duke of Wellington at worship at St Mary's, Walmer in *The Illustrated London News*, September 1852. He faces the enormous pulpit and the chancel is all but ignored. (© Illustrated London News Ltd / Mary Evans Picture Library)

orientation of the church has been rotated to north-south to face the pulpit, rather than west-east, to face the altar. The opening on the left, apparently ignored in this arrangement, is actually the Norman chancel arch, although it is not entirely clear how the chancel might be accessed through the jumble of private pews. Similarly, a photograph taken in the chancel of the church of St Peter and St Paul, Heytesbury (Wiltshire), shortly before its restoration by Butterfield in 1865, shows that elements of the medieval screen have been retained, but only because they have been incorporated into later, botched carpentry, with no other function than to shut off the chancel itself, which appears as not much more than a storeroom (Fig. 2). Just beyond the chancel arch, incidentally, can be seen Lord Heytesbury's family pew – a large raised, private gallery of the type decried as a 'flying pew' by opponents of the appropriated pew system – which no doubt gave a fine view of the pulpit.

In fact, this period probably saw more systematic destruction of the existing medieval screens than any other. And paradoxically, it was just the drive to repair and renew, and to increase the number of 'sittings',

Fig. 2: A photograph of about 1864 taken within the disused chancel at the church of St Peter and St Paul, Heytesbury, before restoration. A rough partition including elements of the former rood screen entirely closes off the chancel. (With the kind permission of St Peter and Paul's Church, Heytesbury)

'sittings', that could lead to the disappearance of screens. In one example, St Nicholas', Tadmarton (Oxfordshire), a plaque records the reseating of the church to provide an additional 100 places, including 70 that were 'free' in 1825. These seats are still present in the church and confirm the former existence of a rood screen, for several of the 1825 benches can be seen to contain carved elements reused from the medieval rood screen's dado (Fig. 3).

Pugin and the promotion of the rood screen

When Sir Gilbert Scott wrote his memoir, between 1866 and 1873, he dismissed his own early churches of the 1830s with contempt, even guiltily wishing they might be burnt down. He was quite explicit in declaring that it required the twin illuminating influences of A.W.N. Pugin and the Cambridge Camden Society (the Ecclesiologists) to open his eyes.[3] This awakening had enabled him to go on to become the most prolific, successful and imitated of Victorian ecclesiastical architects. It is, of course, arguable whether it was just these two influences that led to the absolute transformation of church architecture that took place during the 1840s, '50s and '60s. However, they were certainly the two clearest voices condemning the 'auditory' church and the clearest in defining in purely architectural terms a new kind of church designed around symbolic meaning and intended for essentially sacramental worship centred on the chancel. The significance of this in the context of this chapter is that it was precisely Pugin and the Camdenians, and largely they alone, who actively promoted rood screens, energetically and persistently, in both print and in concrete architectural expression. Without their intervention many more of the surviving medieval screens would have been lost. And with their promotion of rood screens many new ones came to be created. However, in contrast with the other elements of church planning and design that they promoted, the Camdenians' and Pugin's advocacy of rood screens were a comparative failure. It is this element of their doctrines that defines both the extent and the limits of their respective programmes: for Pugin within Roman Catholicism and for the Ecclesiologists within Anglicanism.

Pugin's best known writings, such as *Contrasts* and *True Principles*,[4] with their call for truth to materials and the subjection of decoration to construction, have been seen by Pevsner and others as a forerunner of modern ideas about architecture.[5] But it was not in *Contrasts* that Scott found his inspiration. It was instead Pugin's two articles in a Roman Catholic periodical, the *Dublin Review*, of 1841 and 1842 that had led Scott to change the course of his architectural work. In these two

Fig. 3: A bench at St Nicholas', Tadmarton incorporates panels reused from the medieval rood screen's dado. The screen was destroyed and the church reseated in 1825. (Photo: John Roberts, 2016)

pieces Pugin set forth a series of examples of the new Roman Catholic churches he was building, to the eyes of his contemporaries both remarkably medieval in character and strikingly modern (Fig. 4). In the brilliant illustrations, which are simultaneously descriptively clear and expressive, Pugin showed that in his hands the Roman Catholic Church was marching ahead in the effective use of gothic in the creation of new church buildings. To those like Scott – groping for an authentic gothic language – they were a revelation. In almost every case, alongside the precisely articulated exteriors, Pugin provided a cross-section showing the chancel arch, and those chancel arches were filled with elaborate rood screens, topped by the Rood group of crucifix flanked by Saints Mary and John.

A particularly fruitful outcome of the notice Pugin's *Contrasts* had achieved was his meeting with Daniel Rock, a Catholic priest deeply immersed in the study of pre-Reformation liturgical practice.[6] Most significantly Rock was chaplain to the Earl of Shrewsbury. One of the richest men in England, this Catholic peer was closely involved in building projects for the Church alongside the work on and around his own seat at Alton in Staffordshire. Deeply impressed by Pugin's astonishing knowledge of gothic forms and his boundless confidence

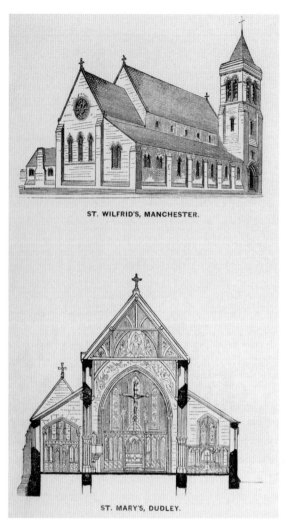

Fig. 4: A selection of A. W. N. Pugin's influential illustrations for his new Roman Catholic church designs in *The Dublin Review* of May 1841, subsequently published in book form as *The Present State of Ecclesiastical Architecture* in 1843. Rood screens are a prominent feature of the interiors. (Plates VIII, XII and VII. Reproduced from https://archive.org)

in employing it, Shrewsbury became Pugin's patron. The result, with Shrewsbury either as his direct employer or as a major financial contributor to the Church's own projects, was a sequence of commissions for Pugin in the late 1830s and early 1840s. The frontispiece for Pugin's *Apology for the Revival of Christian Architecture*, published in 1843, shows no fewer than 25 of Pugin's works from this period, but very few of these churches were completed as Pugin intended, usually for reasons of cost or because of local disagreements about the form they

ST. GEORGE'S FIELDS, LONDON.

were taking. In significant cases, it was Pugin's proposals for ambitious rood screens that became the particular focus for dispute.

An early example was Pugin's commission in 1838 for St Alban's, the new parish church for the rapidly growing town of Macclesfield (Cheshire), after Shrewsbury offered a major financial contribution on the condition that Pugin should replace the existing architect. Pugin's intended tower and spire were never completed and St Alban's design is a strange combination of perpendicular and German influence, with exceptionally high and slender arcades (Fig. 5). Pugin's rood screen was designed, again taking German models, to fill the high chancel arch, and the effect is awkward. The screen, one of the first of the Gothic Revival, is certainly quite unlike the English examples Pugin would soon come to favour. A particular weakness is the flimsy rood loft, which can only

Fig. 5: The rood screen at St Alban's, Macclesfield, conceived by Pugin in around 1838 and in place by 1841. One of the first of Pugin's screens, it is a tentative and insubstantial design, surmounted by a genuine sixteenth-century German rood group donated by Pugin. (Photo: John Roberts, 2017)

be approached by a precipitous arrangement of ladder and platform in the south chapel. One valuable legacy for the church, however, is the Rood group, genuine German work of around 1500 that Pugin had acquired on his travels, restored and re-coloured by him, and donated to the church.

A second example is St Chad's, Birmingham: a major new church for the rapidly expanding metropolis, and now the Catholic cathedral. It was built between 1839 and 1841, and was subject to arguments about expense from the first. Pugin's similarly ambitious church at Derby was approaching completion at the time at about double his original estimate. At Birmingham, partly for cost-control and partly because Pugin's promotion of his own version of the needs of the Catholic liturgy had little support from the senior clergy, the church authorities tried to exclude Pugin's proposed rood screen. It only remained in the plans at Shrewsbury's insistence. A much larger church than that at Macclesfield, St Chad's was again of brick in a German style, and again its crossing tower and spire were never completed. Much of Pugin's interior decoration has been swept away in the twentieth century, including the splendid rood screen. Its much curtailed remains now grace a small Anglican church in Reading, precisely the type of cheap chapel of ease that Pugin so despised (Fig. 6).

Pugin's masterpiece is St Giles', Cheadle (Staffordshire) (Fig. 7). A few miles from Shrewsbury's seat at Alton, it was built from 1840 to 1846 and was commissioned, and directly paid for, by Shrewsbury himself, with the result there was little interference from the Catholic authorities. No expense was spared, although the final payments had to be wrung from the Earl who had come to baulk at the huge costs, which by 1846 had risen from an initially generous estimate of £5,000 to a staggering £40,000.

Pugin was searching in these churches for an artistic mastery of space, volume and proportion that would equal the clarity of his vision about how architecture should serve Catholic theology and liturgy. A great step forward came with his abandoning Continental in favour of entirely English medieval idioms. Nowhere was this more clearly expressed than at Cheadle where Pugin had a free hand to create his ideal Catholic parish church for an English context. The result is spectacular, from the spire which completely upstages the nearby medieval Anglican church to its remarkable interior, complete with rood screen and Rood group. Pugin visited East Anglia in 1840 while conceiving the design, and again in April 1844 specifically to see details of medieval screen decoration. He wrote to Shrewsbury from Norfolk: 'I am half frantic

Fig. 6: The remnants of the screen designed by Pugin for St Chad's, Birmingham, 1841, now installed in much-reduced form at Holy Trinity, Reading. (Photo: John Roberts, 2016)

Fig. 7: Pugin's finest rood screen, at St Giles', Cheadle of 1844. In English fifteenth-century style, it forms the centrepiece of an interior of unparalleled richness. (Photo: John Roberts, 2016)

with delight. I have seen churches with the painting & gilding nearly perfect!!!! Such screens. Exquisite painting. I shall have such glorious authorities for Cheadle'.[7]

Screens were a central element in the interior richness of St Giles' and the large Rood was effectively the centrepiece of the church. It may be because Pugin accepted some need for economy at these later stages of the work that the rood screen, although gorgeously painted and gilded, did not have the painted images on the dado that Pugin had earlier intended. It may also be that he just did not trust any artist to achieve the medieval effect he wanted, for to match the honest crudeness of the Norfolk originals would have been difficult without falling into pastiche.

The church and its interior immediately aroused great interest, among Protestant churchmen and architects as well as Catholics. It was widely reported, usually with enthusiasm, and the new *Illustrated London News* devoted two full pages and seven illustrations to it, saying: 'Probably so perfect a church was never erected in England before, as there is a completeness in the building which defies words to express, or representations to give an idea of'.[8] Although Pugin continued to receive Catholic commissions, for abbeys, churches in Ireland, schools and so on, the high point of his ecclesiastical work had been reached. Much of his time during his final years was taken up with his immense contribution to the Houses of Parliament, which he regarded as hack work and for which he received little recognition at the time. The Catholic church's reluctance to employ him was their loss. One rather lovely screen from 1846, which he designed for the small Catholic Church of St Peter's, Marlow (Buckinghamshire) for a wealthy young Catholic convert, is unusually of stone (Fig. 8). There was also one important restoration of an Anglican church at St Mary the Virgin, Wymeswold, (Leicestershire) where Pugin designed a new chancel screen for a Camdenian incumbent. One telling feature of this screen, which is a very confident and simple design, is that Pugin completely ignored the surviving fragments of the dismantled medieval rood screen, which were (and still are) in the church in favour of a completely new design. This is one of Pugin's very few Anglican church commissions, for he was largely shunned by Anglicans afraid of being accused of Popery, as with his aborted project for new buildings at Balliol College, Oxford, where there was dismay that the college could even think of using this Catholic to build on a site 'opposite where the martyr's fires had burned'.

To Pugin's disgust and dismay, the Catholic Church tended through the later 1840s to employ competent architects who could work with

Fig. 8: Pugin's rood screen at St Peter's Roman Catholic church, Marlow of 1845–46, built for a wealthy Catholic convert. Unusually among Pugin's screens, it is of stone.
(Photo: John Roberts, 2018)

Pugin's idioms rather than to hire the man himself, with his reputation for over-spending and his insistence on liturgical features which were not, in their view, his to determine. Some of these ersatz, Puginesque churches are very fine, by architects such as Joseph Hansom and William Wardell, but only occasionally included screens as he would have wanted. Pugin, meanwhile, was increasingly ignored, and when he published his final book *A Treatise on Chancel Screens and Rood Lofts* in 1851,[9] a strong faction in the Catholic Church rose up to condemn him and his espousal of screens in particular. Pugin's *Treatise* was, for him, unusually defensive, for in it he describes the origins, development and function of rood screens through various categories of 'ambonoclasts', or screen destroyers. Beset by failing mental and physical health, Pugin died in rather tragic circumstances soon afterwards in 1852.

The Cambridge Camden Society's rood screens

In addition to Pugin, George Gilbert Scott credited the Damascene conversion of his church architecture to the work of the Cambridge Camden Society – the Ecclesiologists. They too were vigorous promoters of rood screens. This energetic and combative body originated at Cambridge in 1839 when it was founded by a group of undergraduates, most prominently two future clergymen, Benjamin Webb and James Mason Neale. They were joined by Alexander Beresford Hope, who went on to a prominent career in politics, where he supported the High-Church faction through the anti-Ritualist struggles of later decades. He was of particular importance among the Ecclesiologists by practical example, for he had the money to take their ideas into reality. The influential president of the Society in its early years, who contributed a much-needed moderating influence, was Thomas Thorp, senior tutor at Trinity College who was also Archdeacon of Bristol.

Founded almost simultaneously with the Oxford Society for the Promotion of Gothic Architecture, the Cambridge Camden Society outspokenly asserted authority over the form which restored or new Anglican churches should take. That there was a gasping thirst for such advice was proved during the first years of their existence by the remarkable success of a sequence of their publications offering in uncompromising – even immoderate – terms detailed programmes for what should and should not be done by church restorers and church builders. Their pamphlets, such as *A Few Words to Churchwardens*,[10] were taken up in their thousands by parishes across England. Their magazine *The Ecclesiologist*, which offered articles and reviews on church architecture and church fittings, continued to be published until 1868. It provides a thorough, even if thoroughly biased, view of the progress of the Gothic Revival in ecclesiastical architecture through almost three decades.

Underlying the advice they propounded was a theology, closely related to that of the Oxford Movement, that defined the essential characteristic of worship, and the architectural space it was to occupy, as 'Sacramentality'. Neale and Webb defined this concept as 'the idea that, by the outward and visible form, is signified something inward and spiritual: that the material fabrick symbolizes, embodies, figures, represents, expresses, answers to, some abstract meaning.'[11] In relation to the symbolism of the rood screen, they were quite specific, and Pugin had used the identical formulation: the nave contained the congregation, and represented the Church Militant, whereas the chancel represented the Church Triumphant. The chancel was the location for the prime sacrament of holy communion, and was entered via the rood screen, which traditionally supported the Rood group of crucifix, Mary and John. The rood screen thus represented Christ's passion, through which the salvation of the congregation became possible.[12]

In addition to this symbolic role of the rood screen in the eucharistic interpretation of worship, the rood screen defined physically the separation of a sacerdotal priesthood. It emphasized their special status by defining emphatically the chancel as an area reserved for the celebrants. The Camdenians were promoting 'a compound of dogmatic theology gleaned from the [Oxford Movement] Tractarians and dogmatic architectural theory gleaned from Pugin'.[13] And according to J. Mordaunt Crook, by 1867 'the triumph of ecclesiology was incontestable … a group of Cambridge undergraduates had succeeded in transforming the appearance of every Anglican church in the world'.[14] Churches had indeed changed in the direction the Ecclesiologists were demanding, with separated, coherent spaces for nave, chancel and sanctuary, rising on a series of steps, and with seating re-orientated towards the chancel. Most centrally placed three-decker pulpits had been cut down in size and moved to the side of the chancel arch. The process of removing galleries and private box pews, and their replacement with open, eastward-facing benches was well under way. The architecture, following liturgical practice, had changed from the 'auditory' service, centred on the pulpit and the sermon, to the 'sacramental', centred on the chancel and the eucharist.

While they were accused by their opponents on the Evangelical wing of the church of undisguised Popery, the Cambridge Camdenians insisted that they were actually pursuing an ideal of church architecture appropriate for Anglican worship that had been a part of the religious settlement that followed the Reformation and had been confirmed by the reforms of Archbishop Laud. It is a paradox that a particularly vocal enemy most accurately defined their position in relation to the Oxford Movement, which had created the climate in which they flourished. In his widely read sermon, published in 1844 as *The Restoration of Churches is the Restoration of Popery*, the Revd Francis Close of Cheltenham, while hurling accusations of idolatry and superstition, showed remarkably perceptive observations of both the connection and the difference between the Oxford Tractarians and the Cambridge Camdenians. Romanism was taught, 'analytically' at Oxford, he said, and 'artistically' at Cambridge. Significantly, Close chose the Camdenians' support for rood screens as the most egregious example of the dangers inherent in their approach: '[The Ecclesiologists argue that] the chancel to be carefully separated from the nave by a Roodscreen.' So furnished, the Chancel is declared to be 'the Holy of Holies into which the unilluminated are not to be introduced' – 'it is a severe and awful solitude' – in a word, the east wall is the place for the altar – the Chancel for the priests – the Nave 'for the people'. By asserting the chancel as the exclusive province of the priesthood, separated by a closed screen, they were surrendering the gains of the Reformation.[15]

The Camdenian enthusiasm for rood screens can be found in virtually every one of their publications through the 1840s. Surviving screens were to be protected at all costs. New churches would be 'unreal' without one. This enthusiasm found dramatic physical expression around 1840 when the young Beresford Hope took his Camdenian principles to the church his father, a retired Peninsular War general, was building on his estate at Kilndown in Kent with Anthony Salvin as architect. Aged around 20, Hope oversaw the completion of the church, which was in essence a simple rectangular box modelled on the solemn little church at Littlemore that Newman had built when he retreated from Oxford controversies in 1835. Christ Church, Kilndown had similar proportions to Littlemore, a comparable spindly hammer-beam roof, western entrance and triple window at the east end. There the similarities ended, for the young Hope determined to impart a quite different character to the church. The most notable feature of his interior is the chancel screen (Fig. 9). Whereas Littlemore in its original form had no chancel, Hope at Kilndown used the screen to create one, albeit much shallower than would soon become the norm. The screen is a remarkable example of craftsmanship, surely one of the finest pieces of woodwork of its period in England. It was designed by Richard

Cromwell Carpenter, who was to become one of the Camdenians' favourite architects, and was certainly in place by 1845. It follows Pugin's examples in the addition of a holy text but is otherwise quite distinct, in perpendicular style, and beautifully carved and coloured.

The Ecclesiologists continued to promote rood screens throughout the 1840s and 1850s. Through their efforts very many medieval examples were protected during the wave of 'restorations', many of dubiously destructive character, that swept through the parishes of England during this period. In their insistence that new churches should contain a rood screen, on the other hand, they were less successful, for Church authorities frequently saw the rood screen as an expression of controversial Tractarian and Romanist leanings. As an essentially optional fitting, the rood screen frequently became the feature that could most easily be excluded, and the peace thus maintained.

In such circumstances the great majority of new churches were built without a rood screen and the presence of one in a church built in this period is generally an indication of the local influence of the Ecclesiologists. A good example is St Nicholas', Kemerton

Fig. 9: The rood screen at Christ Church, Kilndown was the first Camdenian rood screen, designed for Beresford Hope by R. C. Carpenter before 1845. The design and carving are of outstanding quality – see the linenfold panelling (*inset*). (Photo: John Roberts, 2018)

Fig. 10: Carpenter was responsible for the extensive restoration, effectively a rebuilding, of St Nicholas', Kemerton for Archdeacon Thorp, the Cambridge Camden Society's president. The rood screen dates from 1847 and is in the more sober thirteenth-century style that was by now favoured by the Ecclesiologists. (Photo: John Roberts, 2018)

(Worcestershire) – the church restored by the Society's president Archdeacon Thorp at his own parish (Fig. 10). Thorp was granted the living in support of his role as Archdeacon of Bristol and carried out substantial restoration, in large part a rebuilding, in 1846–7. The chosen architect was Carpenter and the church is in the decorated style of the early fourteenth century, by this time the form of gothic favoured by the Ecclesiologists. It is one of the finest early Victorian country churches. There is a long chancel with the requisite stepped arrangement and sedilia and piscina, separated from the nave by an oak screen with fine wrought-iron gates which, like the church's excellent lighting corona, may be by the firm of Hardman, closely connected with Pugin. The chancel has lateral stalls returned against the east side of the screen for Thorp's surpliced choir, one of the first in a village church. The screen itself is unpainted and in decorated style, a double move away from Carpenter's earlier perpendicular screen at Kilndown. There is a Latin inscription on the cornice, reading 'Per Crucem et Passionem tuam Libera nos Domine'. The reference to the Passion emphasises the theology of the rood screen as described by Neale and Webb, even in the absence of a surmounting Rood.

As they joined their parishes, several other Camdenian clergymen took their allegiance with them from Cambridge, building churches in the correct Ecclesiological manner, including rood screens. In November 1844, G. H. Hodson, a fellow of Trinity College, Cambridge, member of the Cambridge Camden Society from late 1840 and a committee member from 1843, came to the parish of Cookham Dean in Berkshire as curate and took charge of the project to build the new church of St John the Baptist. Carpenter was again the architect and the church was built in 1844–5. The simple oak screen has plainly cusped decorated tracery supported on turned and ringed shafts, entirely typical for Ecclesiologically correct churches of the period, and can be taken as a model for the kind of simple screen the Ecclesiologists wanted introduced in all new churches built with limited funds (Fig. 11).

An especially important example of a new church of the 1840s which combined Tractarian connections with Camdenian architecture was St Paul's, Brighton (East Sussex), the plans described with 'warm approbation' in The Ecclesiologist in April 1846, not least because there was to be 'a good screen'. The church was founded as a chapel of ease and largely funded by the Vicar of Brighton, Henry Michell Wagner, a well-connected, wealthy, old-fashioned High-Churchman, who built a number of churches in a variety of styles in the rapidly growing town. The fourth of these was St. Paul's and it was to be one of the most significant churches built on the Camdenian model. It was founded in a poor area of Brighton with the intention that Wagner's son Arthur Douglas Wagner would be its first perpetual curate. A. D. Wagner was at Trinity College in the early 1840s and joined the Cambridge Camden Society in 1842. He took a strong interest in the building of St Paul's and it was probably his influence that led to the appointment of Carpenter as architect. He seems to have taken great interest in the fitting out of the church. In addition to his Cambridge Camden background, the younger Wagner became closely connected with the Oxford Movement, knowing Newman, Manning and Keble well and with Pusey as a close friend. Because he put his Tractarian sympathies into practice, he became a prominent target for anti-Ritualist attack from the 1860s.

St Paul's was Carpenter's first important town church, built from 1846 to 1848. It was in decorated style and seems surprisingly spacious

Fig. 11: At St John the Baptist, Cookham Dean, of 1845 Carpenter introduced a simple screen with the uprights formed from turned balusters, a design based on the earliest medieval examples, such as that at Stanton Harcourt (Oxfordshire). This easily copied model was widely reproduced. The doors are a later replacement, probably for originals of wrought iron. (Photo: John Roberts, 2018)

given the restricted site. A sense of the original appearance can be gleaned from a print which was made in the early 1850s (Fig. 12). As at Kemerton, the open form of the screen offered a largely uninterrupted view into the chancel. *The Ecclesiologist* in November 1849 took the opportunity in its delighted review of the church to proclaim that 'our principles have triumphed'. The article went on to praise Carpenter as a 'personal friend' who had 'ventured to ally himself with our fortunes, and to run the risk of unpopularity'.

Another particularly significant new church of this period was St Barnabas', Pimlico (London). It was built by William Bennett to serve a poor district on the fringes of his fashionable Knightsbridge parish. Bennett was an energetic and conscientious priest, an enthusiastic follower of the Oxford Movement, but not a member of the Ecclesiological Society. He succeeded in raising the funds for this essentially philanthropic project from his wealthier parishioners, who included the prime minister, Lord John Russell. As well as the church,

Fig. 12: Carpenter's most important town church of St Paul's, Brighton (1846–8). The tracery of the rood screen is of an elaborate Decorated period design, its fine carving intended to allow for maximum transparency while maintaining the required barrier to the chancel. (Reproduced with the kind permission of the Vicar and Churchwardens of St Paul's church, Brighton)

Fig. 13: A contemporary coloured watercolour of St Barnabas, Pimlico, built for the Tractarian William Bennett and consecrated in 1850, shows that it was richly decorated from the first, with a prominent rood screen. It was the most controversial of all Ecclesiological churches and became the focal point for anti-Catholic riots. (With the kind permission of St Barnabas' church, Pimlico)

there was a school for choristers, a house for Bennett himself and accommodation for four additional clergy. The architect was Thomas Cundy II, who was not a close follower of the Ecclesiologists and this church was his most Ecclesiologically correct, showing the influence of Camdenian ideas as promoted by a Tractarian patron. Beresford Hope himself donated the elaborate chancel corona, by Hardman, for the large sum of £90. The interior has subsequently been much elaborated but a watercolour shows that it was richly decorated in its original form, and that the rood screen was a central part of the liturgical scheme (Fig. 13). Reporting on the church in 1850 *The Ecclesiologist* called it the 'most complete, and, with completeness, most sumptuous church that has been dedicated to the use of the Anglican communion since the revival'.[16] The rood screen was singled out for praise, although the cross, itself a highly contentious addition, was thought to be too small.

Evangelical resistance to chancel screens

St Barnabas' is actually more famous for the events that centred on Bennett and the worship in his church than for the architecture itself, although the two were inseparable. It was opened in 1850, the year of the so-called 'papal aggression' when the Pope created the English Roman Catholic episcopacy. Bennett's ritual practices and the novel Oxford Movement character of his church aroused bitter public debate among Anglican divines and politicians. Whipped on by the press, the controversy drew at first curious crowds and subsequently angry mobs, and it soon became a focus for anti-Catholic rioting over an extended period.

The events in Pimlico were a violent early skirmish in the anti-Ritualist controversy that was to trouble the Church for the rest of the century. In the early stage, the form of the fitting out of churches was as likely as the ritual practices of the clergy involved to give rise to opposition. The Cambridge Camden Society had already courted disaster with their restoration of the Round Church in Cambridge, where in 1845 they lost an expensive legal process in defence of their new stone altar. The society was almost bankrupted and was forced to quit Cambridge for London. From then they went by the new name of The Ecclesiological Society. Roodscreens were becoming a particular focus for opposition. Robert Liddell, Bennett's successor at Pimlico, was taken to court by Evangelical parishioners for his supposedly Romish 'innovations', which included the cross above the rood screen. Bennett himself had been forced to resign and was found a potentially quieter parish at Frome in Somerset. There he got into further trouble over his

Fig. 14: Holy Innocents, Highnam was designed by Henry Woodyer for Thomas Gambier Parry, a leading Ecclesiologist. The rood screen of c.1850 was deprived of 'holy doors' in its original form on the orders of the bishop. (Photo: John Roberts, 2018)

ritual practices, facing prosecution in 1869. As an indication of a later change in mood, however, he was acquitted in both the Court of Arches and the Privy Council.

Another important Ecclesiological church of around 1850 was Holy Innocents' at Highnam (Gloucestershire), built by the Ecclesiologist Thomas Gambier Parry, with Henry Woodyer as his architect (Fig. 14). Even though he was building the splendid new church with his own money on his own estate, Parry was forced to compromise over the rood screen. Bishop Monk of Gloucester stressed the need of 'avoiding all Romish ornaments … it cannot be justified to provoke outcry and abuse … It is fair to say that if anything popish is detected the abuse will fall not upon you, but upon me …'.[17] As a result, Gambier Parry was compelled to omit the 'holy doors' to the rood screen that were so essential to complete the separation of the chancel demanded by Ecclesiological dogma.

By this time the Ecclesiologists were having to accept defeat on the question of rood screens. Bishop Philpotts of Exeter, who had been a consistent supporter and was encouraging the restoration of several of Devon's splendid medieval rood screens, admitted that he could no longer insist on rood screens in new churches. *The Ecclesiologist* acknowledged that they had suffered 'more obloquy' for rood screens than for any other thing they had advocated.[18] In Evangelical Bristol, Thorp as Archdeacon in 1849 had succeeded in having only one new church – St Jude's, Pointz Pool – built with a rood screen in correct Ecclesiological style, but in 1851 a new incumbent bowed to local pressure and its 'holy doors' were removed and converted into a reading desk in the nave, a feature particularly despised by the Ecclesiologists.[19]

In London Bishop Blomfield in trying to restrain Tractarian influence in the city actively intervened in a number of instances. Edward Stuart, a wealthy young Oxford-educated clergyman and a committee member of the Ecclesiological Society, was building the major church of St Mary Magdalene, Munster Square, once again in a poor district attached to his parish. In 1852 *The Ecclesiologist* congratulated Carpenter, the architect, for making the most of a hostile situation by designing a fine low stone wall, sometimes referred to as *cancelli*, across the chancel arch in place of the full screen that the bishop was refusing to sanction.[20] This presaged the change that was to lead to low stone chancel walls replacing rood screens *faute de mieux* as an acceptable alternative. William Butterfield, himself becoming one of the Ecclesiologists' favoured architects, helped lead the way. In the most famous of all the Ecclesiologists' churches, All Saints, Margaret Street, the bishop's resistance to rood screens

Fig. 15: All Saints, Margaret Street
was the most influential of the
churches built by an Ecclesiologist,
in this case Beresford Hope himself.
William Butterfield's superb low
chancel screen of marble and
coloured stone, with elaborate
metal doors, was in place by 1851.
It became the acceptable model
when rood screens of full height
were forbidden, in this case by
Bishop Blomfield.
(Photo: John Roberts, 2016)

compelled Beresford Hope, who provided most of the funds, against his wishes to accept a low stone wall and gates rather than a full rood screen (Fig. 15).[21] But, as well as securing the desired separation of the chancel, Butterfield showed what a magnificent effect even a low stone screen could achieve.

Another low screen by Butterfield from this period is worth noting to show the versatility of the compromise form in churches of different scales. At the small church of St Mary's, Wavendon (Buckinghamshire) of 1848–9, Butterfield introduced an inexpensive low screen, richly coloured, and with fine 'holy doors', brightly painted (Fig. 16). Architects were exploiting the decorative potential offered by the low screens that were now replacing the severity of the earlier wooden Ecclesiological screens. Frequently, the low stone screen became the preferred arrangement in grander new churches too, fulfilling the Tractarian or Ecclesiological desire for a barrier to the chancel while satisfying the counter demand that the view into and the sound from the chancel should be unimpeded. G. E. Street's low stone screens contributed

ambitious effects in his pursuit of dramatic polychromatic design in the high Victorian period: for example, at St Peter's, Bournemouth (Dorset) of 1864 (Fig. 17), where there is the additional feature, not uncommon, of metalwork railings on top of the screen, increasing the separation without introducing any barrier to sight or hearing. The incumbent was a Tractarian, and the church was built along Ecclesiological lines.

The restoration of medieval screens

By the late 1860s, the leading architects had gained sufficient confidence and facility in their use of gothic forms themselves to determine what should be done in church restorations. The balance had shifted away from essentially advisory bodies such as the Ecclesiologists. Where a medieval screen survived, antiquarian or archaeological appreciation suggested that it should be retained and restored. If there was none, it was entirely optional whether a new one should be created, the outcome depending on the availability of funds and the liturgical leanings of the patrons and clergy. This does not mean that existing medieval screens

Fig. 16: At St Mary's, Wavendon in 1849 Butterfield showed the potential for low chancel screens in churches with more limited funds than were available at Margaret Street – here stone and plaster enhanced by rich colour and highly-designed metalwork.
(Photo: John Roberts, 2018)

135

Fig. 17: At St Peter's, Bournemouth (1866) Street topped a low alabaster chancel screen with elaborate ironwork to achieve simultaneous separation and transparency. (Photo: John Roberts, 2019)

were entirely immune from destruction, particularly if they were in severely damaged or fragmentary condition. In his role as Diocesan Architect from 1850, G. E. Street reviewed all the plans to restore or build churches in the Oxford diocese. His reports, which survive, often show him attempting to preserve screens where the restorers had no intention of keeping them. As many chancel arches were entirely redesigned and rebuilt during restoration a number of screens were lost in the process. Often rood screens were moved from the chancel arch to a less prominent position, perhaps across the tower arch as at St Mary's, Garsington or as the entrance to a chapel, as at St Leonard's, Sunningwell (both in Oxfordshire). That losses continued is revealed by the detailed descriptions of churches in the neighbourhood of Oxford published by the Oxford Society for the Promotion of Gothic Architecture in 1846.[22] Eight of the screens described are still in place, but six have gone and one was moved to a chapel.

Radical restoration was by this time widespread and it is important to recognise that most apparently medieval screens consist only of what nineteenth century restorers have permitted us to see. While some restoration could be clumsy and distort the medieval character of screen remains, in other cases very fine work was done. At St Disen's, Bradninch (Devon) the fine painted screen was restored under the auspices of the Exeter Architectural Society in 1853, with a significant financial contribution from the Ecclesiological Society (Fig. 18). At St Mary's, Adderbury (Oxfordshire) where G. G. Scott restored the screen in 1870 the medieval tracery had to be retrieved from storage for the screen to be re-erected. The vaulting and loft, however, are largely Scott's creation (Fig. 19).

A good example to show the problems involved in interpreting an apparently medieval screen is St. Mary's, Bloxham (Oxfordshire). This major church was restored with an admirably light touch by Street in 1865–6 and the screen as we see it also dates from then (Fig. 20). The parish records show that the choice of Street came as a result of a

Fig. 18: Bishop Phillpotts of Exeter encouraged the retention and restoration of the fine medieval rood screens of Devon – here at St Disen's, Bradninch where the restoration was overseen by the Exeter Architectural Society in 1853. (Photo: John Roberts, 2016)

Fig. 19: The rood screen at St Mary's, Adderbury was restored, with many of the missing parts reimagined, by George Gilbert Scott in 1870. Despite his later reputation for destructive restoration Scott's work on old screens often showed sensitivity in re-creating them for contemporary worship. (Photo: John Roberts, 2014)

strong recommendation from the bishop. Street's specifications to the tradesmen repeat the bishop's requirement that great care was to be taken to preserve as much as possible in restoring this beautiful and historic church. The faculty granted in 1864 includes the stipulation that the screen should be 'restored to its ancient position'. So where was it? Street's instructions to the carpenter of 1865 tell us that it was at that time dismantled and stored in the parvise – the room over the porch. The old tracery and cusping were to be carefully restored, with a minimum of recarving, with a new moulded cornice and perforated spandrels, and repainting to match the old.[23] Thanks to Street's instruction, the medieval paintings of the Fathers of the Church alternating with symbols of the Evangelists, with their fascinating evidence of sixteenth century iconoclasm, were preserved without repainting, despite their much damaged condition. The subsequent bills from the carpenter, however, and his remarks in justification for exceeding his estimate, show that much more had to be done to the upper part of the screen than was originally envisaged. In its medieval form, the screen had been vaulted

Fig. 20: The much-damaged medieval screen at St Mary's, Bloxham, brought back into use from its dismantled and damaged condition by G. E. Street in 1856. (Photo: John Roberts, 2013)

to carry the rood loft, hence the need for new spandrels in place of the missing vaulting. But the carpenter also explained that in practice he had had to remake 'all the carved heads and panels but one'. The 'cornices, mouldings, spandrels, part of the sill, standards etc' were all worked on. The question must be raised: how much is original? 'Carved heads and panels', seems to mean the tracery. The merging of a fleur-de-lys pattern into the tracery is unique. That this is part of the heraldic crest of Eton College, which by the nineteenth century held the advowson and was a major donor to Street's restoration of the chancel, suggests that it may be a new design by Street in honour of the college. So the screen as we see it, with redesigned tracery, no vaulting or loft, and entirely renewed colouring, is certainly not as it appeared in the middle ages – despite the stated intention to preserve as much as possible.

Two drawings in the parish archive show that the cross above the screen was added a little later, in 1871 to designs by Arthur Hodgson of London. The drawings are separated in date by two weeks and the difference between the first version and that executed is limited to the removal of the Evangelists' symbols from the arms of the cross, precisely the formulation favoured by Pugin and the Ecclesiologists. Although there is no accompanying correspondence, the implication must be that residual nervousness on the part of the incumbent secured the absence of the symbols seen in the first design.

Rood screens revived

George Gilbert Scott himself subscribed to the prevailing view that where there was a screen he would defend it, but if there were none he did not believe it necessary or desirable to create one anew. In his work on reordering cathedrals, however, he did much to promote the idea of new screens, both as an important contribution to making the cathedrals suitable for modern ceremonial worship and as significant aesthetic embellishments. These are not the subject of this paper and are a study in themselves, but their development by Scott did much to revive enthusiasm for screens in parish churches by overcoming the opprobrium they had incurred during the anti-Papist fervour of the 1850s. His cathedral choir screens, among the most richly fanciful examples of High Victorian design, progressed from his early attempts to match the surviving medieval choir stalls at Ely, of 1849–52, to the more adventurous screens he designed with Francis Skidmore as his manufacturer at, for example, Hereford and Salisbury, of 1862 and 1870 respectively (Fig. 21). Regrettably, the latter two were removed during the mid-twentieth century reaction to anything too overtly Victorian

Fig 21: Two of G. G. Scott's influential cathedral choir screens.
Above: Hereford, 1862.
(Photo: Library of Congress, https://www.loc.gov/item/2002696800/)
Below: Ely, 1849–52.
(Photo: John Roberts, 2017)

in appearance. Similar screens by Scott remain in place, however, at Lichfield and Worcester. Apart from their ornate, technical brilliance, the principal characteristic of these screens was their deliberate transparency. It was difficult to object that they obstructed the view into, and the sound from, the choir and high altar.

There are a few screens of this specific type in parish churches, and there is a fine example, also designed by Scott, made by Hardman & Co, at the church of St Michael and All Angels, Clifton Hampden (Oxfordshire) of 1864 (Fig. 22). It replaced Scott's earlier screen in the church of 1844, which was more authentically medieval in appearance. In a few cases even more transparent ironwork screens appeared, as at St Mary the Virgin, Freeland (Oxfordshire) by J. L. Pearson of 1871, again without medieval precedent.

Fig. 22: The iron and brass screen at St Michael and All Angels, Clifton Hampden, designed by G. G. Scott in the manner of his cathedral screens and made by Hart & Co in 1864. (Photo: John Roberts, 2016)

Controversy around rich ceremonial in worship continued through the rest of the century, generally as a struggle between 'Ritualist' and 'anti-Ritualist' camps. A succession of wearisome legal cases failed to resolve differences over acceptable liturgical practice or even to assert a set of commonly observed or enforceable rules. The intervention of Parliament with the Public Worship Regulation Act of 1874 failed in this respect. Whereas Francis Close and his followers had feared that the restoration of churches was the restoration of Popery, by now the fact of restoration and the broadly Ecclesiological layout of churches was generally accepted. Outrage was focused on supposed 'innovations' in the performance of the service: for example, the choice of vestments, using lighted candles, mixing wine and water in the chalice, the celebrant facing eastwards and the use of wafer bread. As the century progressed many bishops tended towards latitude, and greater freedom prevailed for High-Churchmen and Anglo-Catholics to fit out their churches out as they pleased. The symbolic significance of rood screens slipped from awareness, and with it opposition to them lost its force.

Several of the severe screens of the 1840s and 1850s were expanded and elaborated in an atmosphere of greater tolerance and growing enthusiasm for decorative effects. Two of the examples already shown were remodelled in this way: the screen at St Paul's, Brighton was recoloured, with saints painted on the dado, under G. F. Bodley in 1870 (Frontispiece). Bodley also added the vaulting and cresting in the 1880s. That the decorative potential of such a screen had overtaken the theological imperatives is suggested by the fact that the 'holy doors', reused from the earlier screen, were rehung to open outwards – a theological error that would have outraged the Ecclesiologists. In another example, Cundy's screen at St Barnabas', Pimlico, was entirely replaced with a much more elaborate version in 1892, again by Bodley (Fig. 23). Here only Hardman's fine doors from Cundy's screen were retained. With the addition of vaulting, crosses and recolouring, and more elaborate tracery, the effect generally sought was altogether more decorative.

The solemn functionality of the early period had been replaced by a sheer joy in the ornamental potential of such a screen. Doctrinal latitude or even liberalism on the part of the bishops allowed architectural designers the freedom to introduce screens as a contributor to their intended overall aesthetic effect. High-Churchmen leant towards rich, decorative interiors. Anglo-Catholics, successors to the Tractarian mantle, would take this to greater extremes. As funds became available, they would add further and yet more elaboration. St Augustine's, Kilburn was built by J. L. Pearson for the Revd R. C. Kilpatrick in 1870–7.

Fig. 23: Bodley replaced Thomas Cundy II's screen of 1850 at St Barnabas', Pimlico, with a richly decorated version in 1892, topped by a cross bearing Christ in Glory and angels.
(Photo: John Roberts, 2019)

This committed High-Churchman, a friend of the Tractarian leader Edward Pusey, had split away from the Evangelical parish where he was curate to give voice to his desire for a church that adequately expressed the glory of God. When there were objections from some parishioners to his Anglo-Catholic ceremonial, Bishop Tait responded that it was not desirable that the customs of all churches should be the same. As if Pearson's splendour were not enough, in 1890 Kilpatrick added the extraordinary screen, carved by S. J. Nicholl, a Roman Catholic architect and sculptor (Fig. 24). The panels contain scenes of the passion and the screen is surmounted by an extended Rood group, unthinkable a few decades earlier, with saints such as Longinus and Joseph of Arimathea joining Mary and John at the crucifixion.

Fig. 24: One of the finest screens of the Anglo-Catholic movement, at St Augustine's, Kilburn, designed and carved for an Anglican church in 1890 by the Catholic architect S. J. Nichol. (Photo: John Roberts, 2019)

Fig. 25: R. C. Carpenter's 1849 rood screen at Monkton Wyld was adapted with colouring, additional carving and most significantly with a complete rood group by F. C. Eden in about 1888 – converting it into the screen the Ecclesiological architect would have created if he had been permitted.
(Photo: John Roberts, 2016)

As a final example of the greater freedom architects and Anglo-Catholic churchmen later in the century had to make churches as they wished, St Andrew's, Monkton Wyld (Dorset) has a fine screen, coloured, and surmounted with a full Rood group (Fig. 25). The church was built in 1848–9 by Carpenter in a fully Ecclesiological manner. However, the interior decoration owes much to an incumbent later in the century, the Revd J. Maher Camm, who commissioned the altar rail, pulpit and screen between 1886 and 1888. The screen was painted and gilded by F. C. Eden, but the style of the tracery shows that he only elaborated Carpenter's original screen of 1849. The real departure is the addition of a full Rood group, just as advocated by Pugin for his Roman Catholic churches and almost indistinguishable from them, with the Evangelists' symbols in the arms of the cross. The Ecclesiologists would never have dared to promote such an open target for accusations of superstition and idolatry. Merely to place a plain cross above a screen, without the image of Christ, had been enough to bring the Revd Liddell of Pimlico before the ecclesiastical courts in 1855. Now, at the wishes of an Anglo-Catholic incumbent an entirely Puginian Rood group could be added to the earlier screen without drawing controversy, and certainly without incurring prosecution.

Notes

1. A.W. Pugin, *The Ecclesiologist*, January 1845.
2. Michael Port, *600 New Churches: The Church Building Commission 1818-1856*, (Reading, 2006), 98.
3. G. Gilbert Scott (ed.), *Personal and Professional Recollections by the Late Sir George Gilbert Scott*, (1879), 87–88.
4. A.W. Pugin, *Contrasts: or a parallel between the noble edifices of the fourteenth and fifteenth centuries and similar buildings of the present day* (Salisbury, 1836); *The True Principles of Pointed or Christian Architecture*, (1841).
5. Nikolaus Pevsner, *Pioneers of Modern Design: From William Morris to Walter Gropius*, (New Haven and London, 2004), 16 and 42. Pevsner's identification of a linear progression through Pugin, Ruskin and William Morris towards the Bauhaus effectively ignores the rich progression of Victorian ecclesiastical architecture which showed no such direction.
6. Rock's work on the details of Catholic liturgy in the medieval period lent strength to Pugin's work in contrast to the post-Tridentine interpretations demanded by the Church itself: Daniel Rock, *Hierurgia; or the Holy Sacrifice of the Mass, with Notes and Dissertations elucidating its Doctrines and Ceremonies, and Numerous Illustrative Plates, &c.*, (1833).

7. Pugin to Lord Shrewsbury, 25 April 1844. Quoted in Michael Fisher, *'Gothic for Ever': A.W. N. Pugin, Lord Shrewsbury, and the Rebuilding of Catholic England*, (Reading, 2012), 204.

8. *The Illustrated London News*, 9 January 1847, 28–9.

9. A.W. Pugin, *A Treatise on Chancel Screens and Rood Lofts: their antiquity, use, and symbolic signification*, (1851).

10. The Cambridge Camden Society, *A Few Words to Church Builders*, (Cambridge, 1841).

11. W. Durandus, *The Symbolism of Churches and Church Ornaments: a translation of the first book of the Rationale Divinorum Officiorum, written by William Durandus, sometime Bishop of Mende, with introductory essay, notes, and illustrations, by The Rev. John Mason Neale, B.A., and The Rev. Benjamin Webb, B.A., of Trinity College, Cambridge*, (Leeds, 1843), xxvi.

12. 'Remarks on the Church Schemes', in *A Few Hints on the Practical Study of Ecclesiastical Architecture and Antiquities for the Use of the Cambridge Camden Society*, fourth edition, (Cambridge, 1843), 26.

13. Chris Brooks, *The Gothic Revival*, (1999), 246.

14. J. M. Crook, *The Dilemma of Style*, (1987), 63.

15. Revd. Francis Close, *The Restoration of Churches is the Restoration of Popery: proved and illustrated from the authenticated publications of the 'Cambridge Camden Society:' A sermon, preached in the parish church, Cheltenham, on Tuesday, November 5th, 1844*, (1844), 4, 18.

16. *The Ecclesiologist*, August 1850, 110–4.

17. Quoted in Tom Fenton, *To Raise a Perfect Monument to Taste: the story behind the building of Holy Innocents Church, Highnam, Gloucestershire*, (Much Wenlock, 2001), 17–18.

18. *Ecclesiologist*, June 1851, 220.

19. *Ecclesiologist*, February 1851, 2.

20. *Ecclesiologist*, June 1852, 167.

21. In a letter to William Dyce of 22 November 1851 Beresford Hope explained that a rood screen had been intended but it was 'waived to please the Bishop'. See Paul Thompson, 'All Saints Church, Margaret Street, Revisited', *Architectural History*, 8, 73–94.

22. Oxford, *A Guide to the Architectural Antiquities in the Neighbourhood of Oxford*, (Oxford, 1846).

23. The documents and accounts relating to the restoration of the screen are in the parish records held at the Oxford History Centre.

Chapter 6

Gallicans versus Romans: Squaring Medievalism with Trent

ANDREW DERRICK

'If any man says he loves pointed architecture, and hates screens, I do not hesitate to denounce him as a liar, for one is inseparable from the other…'. So asserted A. W. N. Pugin in *A Treatise on Chancel Screens and Rood Lofts, their Antiquity, Use and Symbolic Signification* (1851). This was towards the end of a hugely productive but sadly brief life, and Pugin's mind was becoming unbalanced. Sixteen years earlier he had been received into the Catholic Church, which had largely abandoned screens three hundred years earlier. It had also largely abandoned pointed architecture. While Pugin's mission to restore gothic was not unsympathetically received, he was not able to persuade his adopted Church that the revival of screens should be integral to this. This short chapter attempts to set out why this should have been so.

Chancel screens had originally developed in the thirteenth century, following the requirement of the fourth Lateran Council (1215) that a separate space should be formed for the protection of the reserved Blessed Sacrament. Over time screens increasingly included a rood loft, particularly in England, where this arrangement was associated with the Use of Sarum, the predominant model for parish worship in Britain until the Reformation. As other chapters in this volume demonstrate, chancel screens were often retained, and sometimes replaced by new screens, in the worship of the reformed Church of England, although Rood figures were of course banished.

I have called this chapter 'Gallicans versus Romans'. Gallicanism (as its name suggests) had its origins in France, the essence of its thinking encapsulated in the *Declaration of the Clergy of France* (1682). Crudely, this stated that papal authority extended to spiritual matters only, and not those of a temporal or civil nature. It was further limited by the authority of Church Councils and the authority of bishops, whose assent was required if any decrees were to be defined as infallible. The pope was also bound to take account of the canons and customs of particular churches in exercising his authority. By contrast, ultramontanism ('from beyond the mountains', which is to say the Alps) emphasised the prerogatives and powers of the pope. Pugin (whose father was French) was in some senses a Gallican, not so much for holding that papal primacy might be limited by secular powers, but for his view that the customs of local churches should be taken into account in the exercise of papal authority. He had in mind, for example, the desirability of reviving the Use of Sarum, rather than the Roman breviary, which had only been introduced in the time of Queen Mary.[1] In this respect Pugin's thinking was analogous to some of those contemporary High Church Anglicans who sought a *via media* between Protestant autonomy and full *Romanità*. Many 'old Catholics' in England felt similarly. The ultramontane faction would allow no such rapprochement, declaring that 'by divine ordinance, the Roman Church possesses a pre-eminence of ordinary power over every other Church.'[2]

Post-Reformation norms of worship and liturgy were set down at the Council of Trent (1545–1563). This was the Catholic Church's response to the corruptions identified by the Protestant reformers, and provided the spiritual ammunition needed for the fightback. As well as clarifying and restating Catholic doctrine, the Council condemned various Protestant heresies, and oversaw the codification of the Tridentine Mass. This use – with minor variations – was to remain universal for the next 400 years.

Prominent at the Council of Trent was (St) Charles Borromeo, who became Archbishop of Milan in 1566. He prepared a church-building manual, *Instructiones fabricae et supellectilis ecclesiasticae* (*Instructions on Ecclesiastical Building*, 1577), ostensibly for local use but adopted throughout the Church. It went through many re-issues and translations, its directives broadly followed until the Second Vatican Council.

The Council of Trent also reaffirmed the central importance of the sacraments, and in particular the Eucharist, in which Christ is 'really, truly, substantially present' in the consecrated forms – the doctrine of transubstantiation. This reaffirmation was reflected in the renewal of established devotions such as Benediction, where the Blessed Sacrament is exposed in a monstrance on a high altar, surrounded by candles, and the encouragement of relatively new devotions such as the *Quarant' Ore* when, just before the beginning of Lent, the Sacrament is solemnly exposed on the high altar for forty hours. It is not true (as is sometimes maintained) that Trent outlawed chancel screens. Borromeo's *Instructions* had nothing to say about them, although he did recommend screens down the centre of the nave, to separate the sexes. Nevertheless, while there was no formal proscription, chancel screens or rood lofts were increasingly regarded as incompatible with the new emphasis on a visible high altar and tabernacle. The preferred model was now the 'single space' church, exemplified by Vignola's church of the Gesù, Rome, built for the Jesuits in 1568–80 (Fig. 1).

However, screens continued to be built in convents and monasteries, to maintain the enclosure. They also continued to be erected in some cathedrals and parish churches, especially in northern France and the Low Countries. They served several functions: as well as separating the nave and chancel and also (possibly) accompanying a Calvary group, they could be used for preaching, readings from scripture, or as a platform for an organ or choir. They could be used for the display of relics, or have nave altars placed in front of them. In France they were usually called *jubés*, the term derived from the opening words of the medieval prayer *Jube, Domine, benedicere* (Bid, Lord, a blessing), said to have been pronounced by a deacon from the screen or rood loft. A good Renaissance example is at the church of Notre Dame, Arques-la-Bataille, Normandy (Fig. 2). Another is the elaborately-carved alabaster screen from the medieval cathedral of St John at 's-Hertogenbosch in the Netherlands, built in 1610-1613 under the supervision of Coenraed van Norenberch, to replace a screen attacked by Calvinists. In 1629 the city was reconquered by the Protestants and the cathedral turned over to use by the Dutch Reformed Church. However the screen remained and survived largely intact until removed by the Catholic authorities, after the church was restored to them by Napoleon. It eventually found its way to its current home in the Victoria and Albert Museum.

In England of course, no Catholic churches were being built at the time of the Counter-Reformation. Queen Elizabeth I's 1559 Act of Uniformity had abolished the Mass, and public Catholic worship was to remain illegal until the Second Catholic Relief Act of 1791. There were exceptions, a notable one being Inigo Jones's chapel at St James's Palace, built in 1623 by James I in anticipation of the future Charles I's courtship of the King of Spain's daughter. This was remarkable not only as a place of public Catholic worship, but as the first church in England – of any denomination – to be built in a wholly classical style. It followed the Counter-Reformation principle of a single 'all-seeing' undivided space, with the high altar the main focus, and no provision for a screen.

When church building did once again become legal in 1791, there were various continued proscriptions, for example on the use of steeples and bells.[3] Churches built in the immediate post-Relief Act years had a plain, unassertive character, not very different from contemporary Nonconformist chapels. Even when the Gothic Revival got underway,

Fig. 1: Giacomo da Vignola and Giacomo della Porta, the interior of the Church of the Gesù, Rome, built 1658-84. (Photo: Alvesgaspar, Wikimedia Commons, CC BY-SA 4.0)

Fig. 2: Jubé at Notre Dame, Arques-la-Bataille, Normandy (the present organ is modern).
(Photo: Raimond Spekking, Wikipedia Commons, CC BY-SA 4.0)

there was no immediate departure from the single space principle, as seen in the small church of St Peter's, Winchester (1792), commissioned by Dr John Milner, antiquary and future Vicar Apostolic of the Midland District. This perpendicular-style church was designed by Milner's fellow-antiquary John Carter, and although care was taken to replicate gothic detail authentically, no provision was made for a screen.

Indeed, no such provision was made in any public Catholic church until the early 1840s. One might have been expected at Our Lady and St Walstan's, Costessey Hall (Norfolk), built in 1841 for Dr Frederick Husenbeth, chaplain to the Jerningham family, from designs by J. C. Buckler. Dr Husenbeth was also a keen antiquary and indeed Bishop Milner's biographer. According to the account of the opening in *The Tablet*, 'The Missal used at high mass was a venerable black-letter Sarum Missal, written entirely with the pen on vellum, and most richly illuminated, one of the Catholic times, and which belonged to Archbishop Chicheley, and had not been used at the altar for more than three centuries'.[4] Moreover, this was the first post-Reformation Catholic church (in Norfolk at least) built on a two-cell plan of nave and chancel. Here would have been the obvious place for a screen; however, none was provided.

Even Pugin in his early designs did not install screens; at St Mary's, Derby and St Mary's, Uttoxeter (Staffordshire), both opened in 1839, a rood beam was installed at the chancel arch, surmounted by a crucifix – in each case leaving an unobstructed view of a sanctuary within a shallow apse, separated from the nave only by low altar rails. As such, both churches accorded with post-Tridentine principles. In both churches the rood beam takes the form of a four-centred perpendicular-style arch, an innovation without known Tudor precedent. Of Derby, Pugin later wrote, 'I am aware that the church is full of errors. I had not the influence which I now possess when I designed it & I was weak enough in some respects *to truckle to the times* but this will not happen again...'[5]

So who designed the first post-Reformation rood screen in England? Pugin gave the credit to William Railton, better known as the designer of Nelson's Column in Trafalgar Square.[6] In the 1830s, Railton had built a neo-Tudor house for the Catholic convert Ambrose March-Phillips at Grace Dieu Manor, Leicestershire. A chapel was consecrated in October 1837, and visited by Pugin a month afterwards. On seeing it, he tearfully embraced Phillips. Nevertheless, Railton's screen was not quite ecclesiologically 'correct', and Pugin soon replaced it with one of his own design (which in turn was removed in the 1960s).

Pugin's first rood screen in a *public* Catholic church was at St Alban's, Macclesfield (Fig. 3), opened in May 1841 (the same month as the chapel at Costessey). This was one of many commissions sponsored by the Earl of Shrewsbury and, encouraged by Shrewsbury's chaplain Dr Rock, screens hereon became almost literally an article of faith for Pugin. Macclesfield was followed by St Chad's, Birmingham (Fig. 4), which saw the first signs of resistance from the hierarchy. Much

Fig. 3: A. W. N. Pugin, rood screen at St Alban, Macclesfield, opened 1841 (illustration from *The Present State of Ecclesiastical Architecture*, 1843, Plate XI). (Reproduced from https://archive.org.)

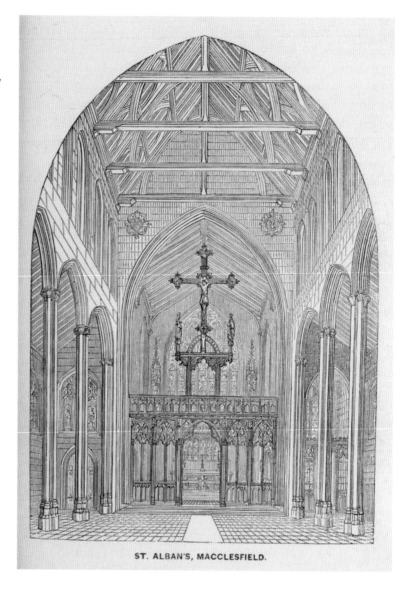

ST. ALBAN'S, MACCLESFIELD.

to Pugin's distress, Bishop Wiseman, coadjutor to the Vicar Apostolic of the Midland District, tried to prevent the screen's installation, and only backtracked when Pugin issued the double threat of resignation and the withdrawal of John Hardman's funding.[7] However, the anti-screen faction were only biding their time.

The apogee of Pugin's ambonophilia was St Giles, Cheadle, Staffordshire (Fig. 5). Here, thanks to Lord Shrewsbury's patronage, none of the financial constraints that bedevilled most of Pugin's Catholic commissions applied. The screen was visually fairly impenetrable, but the reservation of the sacrament in a side chapel made this less

Fig. 4: A. W. N. Pugin, rood screen at St Chad's Birmingham, opened 1841. (© Historic England)

Fig. 5: A. W. N. Pugin, rood screen at St Giles', Cheadle, opened 1846. (Photo: Mark Kirby, 2019)

of a problem. Upon entering this side chapel the convert John Henry Newman, soon to be Pugin's chief adversary, was overcome, murmuring *'porta caeli'*.[8]

The *casus belli* of what became known as the Rood Screen Controversy was the opening of St Wilfrid's, Cotton (Staffordshire). This was to be served by a congregation of Oratorians, headed by Frederick Faber, an associate of Newman and also a convert from Anglicanism. The Oratorians were a post-Reformation order, and Faber was noted for his *Romanità*. However, the site had been given by Lord Shrewsbury, and Pugin prepared designs for a gothic chapel with rood screen. Pugin didn't attend the opening in April 1848, when Mass was said by Wiseman, and Newman preached; he had a more pressing engagement, pursuing a (doomed) courtship. Visiting the church a month later, Pugin was horrified to see that his screen was not in place. Confronting Faber, he was told that it would have interfered with exposition of the Blessed Sacrament; Faber denounced the screen at Cheadle, and said that if he had his way all surviving ancient rood screens would be pulled down and burnt. Newman was called upon to arbitrate, but in the event the Oratorians left Cotton anyway; they were now committed to working in larger towns and cities.[9]

The next salvo was at St Thomas of Canterbury, Fulham, where Pugin installed a screen against the wishes of the donor, Mrs Elizabeth Bowden, who instructed that it be removed. (Mrs Bowden was a friend of Newman, who preached at the opening of the church in June 1848).[10] A month later, Newman did not attend the opening of St George's, Southwark (from 1850 St George's Cathedral, Fig. 6). While Pugin's screen at Birmingham had been a fairly lightweight open structure, more suitable (in his later view) to parochial use, for St George's he designed a fully-blown cathedral screen, a masonry *jubé*. It lasted until 1889.

Pugin's battle with the Oratorians came to a head in 1849, when Fr Faber started work on an improvised chapel in King William Street, off the Strand. Pugin wrote to Lord Shrewsbury:

> Has your lordship heard that the Oratorians have opened the Lowther Rooms as a chapel!! – a place of the vilest debauchery, masquerades etc – one night a MASKED BALL, next BENEDICTUS. … What a degradation for religion. Why, it is worse than the Socialists. … Well may they cry out against screens or anything else. I always said they wanted rooms, not churches, now they have got them. Sad times! I cannot imagine what the world will come to, if it goes on much longer.[11]

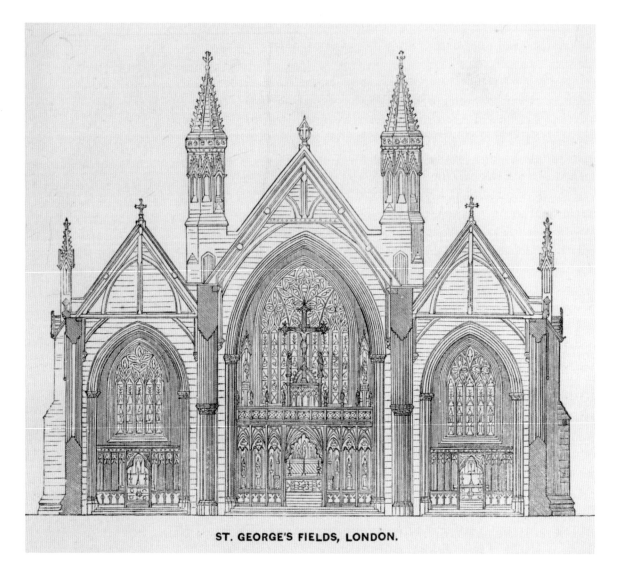

ST. GEORGE'S FIELDS, LONDON.

Fig. 6: A.W.N. Pugin, jubé at St George's, Southwark, opened 1848 (Reproduced from https://archive.org.)

Pugin had an opportunity to show how things should be done properly in his arrangement of the medieval court at the Great Exhibition of 1851. Here the centrepiece was his stone *jubé* for St Edmund's College, Ware (Hertfordshire). 1851 also saw the publication of his *Treatise on Chancel Screens and Rood Lofts*, in which Pugin identified four kinds of 'ambonoclast': the Calvinistic, the Pagan, the Revolutionary, and the Modern. His bitterest words were directed against the last. Referring to the outcry over St George's at Southwark, he wrote:

> Nearly three hundred years have elapsed and the rood was again raised
> in glory in this very city, and the cry 'away with it' was again heard. Came

it from the blaspheming Jews? No. Came it from the bitter Calvinists? No. Came it from the incarnate fiends? No. It proceeded from a modern Catholic ambonoclast!!![12]

Pugin's problem, as Newman wrote to Ambrose March-Phillips, was that 'he has the great fault of a man of genius, as well as the merit. He is intolerant, and, if I might use a stronger word, a bigot.'[13] Some of Pugin's architectural disciples, such as Charles Hansom and William Wardell, were able to install screens in Catholic churches without opprobrium, but the tide was against them, and in the years after the restoration of the hierarchy in 1850, architects sought to work out ways of reconciling gothic forms with the Tridentine principle of the 'all-seeing' church. Joseph Hansom's St Walburge's at Preston (1850-54, Fig. 7) has been described as a Counter-Reformation church in gothic form[14] or, less

Fig. 7: Joseph Hansom, St Walburge's, Preston, 1850-54, the 'flaunting offspring of the unhappy nuptials of Oratorianism and true Christian ecclesiology'. (Photo: Alex Ramsay)

flatteringly by *The Ecclesiologist* (still loyal to Pugin) as 'this flaunting offspring of the unhappy nuptials of Oratorianism and true Christian ecclesiology'.[15] Unhappy or otherwise, screens had no place in this marriage.

In 1857 a new English translation of Borromeo's *Instructions* appeared, written by the architect George Wigley. The illustrations were by the Gothic Revival architect S. J. Nicholl, a pupil of J. J. Scoles, but were of early Christian churches in Rome. Wigley wrote in his preface:

> We hope thus to assist in removing from our English Catholic architecture, the Anglican tendency with which it is threatened; as we should ever endeavour to impress upon ourselves the great fact that we are but a branch (and almost a *new* shoot) from the ever prolific Roman stem.[16]

In the matter of screens, Wigley's translation wrote:

> The image of the Cross, and of Christ our Lord affixed thereon, represented devoutly and properly in wood or other material, should be set up and aptly placed in every church (particularly if it be a parish church) under the very arch of the high chapel … or it may be placed at once on the top of the gate of the railing enclosure of the chapel.[17]

For the avoidance of doubt, Wigley adds in a footnote:

> St Charles describes here the great Crucifix or Rood of a church, without in the least alluding to Rood screens; for when he suggests that this Crucifix may be placed on the gate of the high chapel railing, it must be borne in mind that he describes later enclosures as only 4 ft 1 and a half inches high when made of iron, and as lower still when made of marble or of stone balusters.[18]

Wigley is therefore looking back to the *cancelli* of the Early Christian churches of Rome.

From the mid-1850s, rood screens are seldom encountered in a Catholic context. Ironically enough, the favoured model was established by Pugin's son Edward, none of whose parish churches had screens, apart from one installed – perhaps in filial piety – beneath the rood beam at his father's church at Derby (by Hardman of Birmingham; later removed). E. W. Pugin's church of Our Lady of Reconciliation in Vauxhall, Liverpool (1859-60) solved the problem of the rood screen

Fig. 8: J. F. Bentley, rood loft at Holy Rood, Watford, opened 1890 (Photo: Alex Ramsay)

simply by omitting it, and instead providing hanging Rood figures from the chancel arch, in line with Borromeo's/Wigley's prescription. Visibility was all, and Tridentine principles were reconciled with those of the Gothic Revival. *The Tablet* considered Our Lady of Reconciliation 'a new phase in ecclesiastical architecture' and 'a complete revolution in church building'.[19] Hereon Rood figures, sometimes with a beam but seldom with a screen, became the norm. At Holy Rood, Watford – a significant dedication in this context – J. F. Bentley went a little further and included a rood loft,

> …the largest example erected in this country since Edward VI ordered that all such should be destroyed and burnt.[20]

But again there was no screen (Fig. 8).

Screens do however occasionally put in an appearance, some of them installed by converts from the Church of England, keen to maintain some of the 'Anglican tendency' so deplored by Wigley. Examples include the screen installed by the convert third Marquess of Bute in Charles Hansom's St Peter's at Roath, Cardiff (removed in the 1960s) and (only yards from Pugin's chapel at St Edmund's College), another at St Edmund of Canterbury, Old Hall Green, Hertfordshire, built in 1911 at the expense of Arthur Guy Ellis from designs by the convert architect Arthur Young.

In the twentieth century, the liturgical movement encouraged more active participation of the faithful in the liturgy, with increased emphasis on proximity to, and visibility of, the altar. Gothic, the natural home of the chancel screen, fell out of favour as revived Early Christian and Byzantine styles prevailed, followed by moves (after the Second World War) towards architectural modernism. Needless to say, the documents of the Second Vatican Council (1962–5) had nothing to say about screens, but the liturgical changes that the Council accelerated – separating the tabernacle from the altar, placing the altar in the midst of the people – resulted in the loss of many traditional furnishings, including some of the few surviving rood screens. The most publicised loss was at St Chad's Cathedral, Birmingham, reordered by Weightman & Bullen in 1967–8, with Pugin's screen and Rood figures removed. More recently the figures have been reinstated, while the screen was eventually acquired by Canon Brian Brindley for the Anglican church of Holy Trinity, Reading. Other losses included the screen at St Peter's, Roath, and that designed by Pugin for Ambrose March-Phillips' chapel at Grace Dieu. Even Pugin's own church of St Augustine at Ramsgate

Fig. 9: Restored A. W. N. Pugin screen, St Augustine, Ramsgate (Photo: Marie Muscat-King, 2015)

did not escape, his choir screen removed to a side chapel. However, with the help of national lottery funding, it has recently been reinstated, complete with its medieval Rood figures (Fig. 9). The church is now the Shrine of St Augustine and the National Pugin Centre.

Meanwhile, in 2019 Pope Francis canonised John Henry Newman. Pugin's cause has yet to be advanced.

Notes

Amongst the sources listed below, the writer wishes particularly to acknowledge his debt to Gerard Hyland's essay on the Pugins and J. H. Newman, published in the *Journal of the Pugin Society* (2012).

1. Rosemary Hill, *God's Architect: Pugin and the Building of Romantic Britain,* (2007), 139.
2. Pope Pius IX, *Pastor Aeturnus,* 1870.
3. Bryan Little, *Catholic Churches since 1623,* (1966), 43.
4. *The Tablet,* 5 June 1841, 6.
5. Letter from A. W. N. Pugin to J. R. Bloxam, 24 October 1840, cited in G. Hyland, 'The Pugins, Newman and the Tridentine liturgical rubrics', *True Principles, The Journal of The Pugin Society,* IV no. iii (Spring 2012), 233.
6. Hill (2007), 174.
7. Roderick O'Donnell, *The Pugins and the Catholic Midlands,* (Leominster, 2002), 59.
8. Letter of 21 July 1846 to Elizabeth Bowden, cited in Hyland (2012), 228.
9. Hill (2007), 398-399. For a full account of Pugin's dispute with Newman, see Hyland, (2012), 225–254.
10. Hill (2007), 398.
11. Cited in P. F. Anson, *Fashions in Church Furnishings 1840-1940,* (1960), 39–40.
12. A. W. N. Pugin, *A Treatise on Chancel Screens and Rood Lofts,* (1851).
13. Letter of 15 June 1848, cited in Hyland, (2012), 233.
14. Peter Howell and Ian Sutton, *Faber Guide to Victorian Churches,* (1990).
15. *The Ecclesiologist,* no.89, April 1852, 109.
16. G. J. Wigley, *St Charles Borromeo's Instructions on Ecclesiastical Buildings,* (1857), viii.
17. Wigley, (1857), 27.
18. ibid.
19. *The Tablet,* 1 October 1859.
20. Winefride de l'Hôpital, *Westminster Cathedral and its Architect* (c.1919), 438.

Chapter 7

'A considerable devotional and artistic asset' or an 'obstruction to worshippers'? Changing Perspectives on Chancel Screens in the Twentieth Century

CLARE PRICE

The twentieth century saw a huge variety in new-build church design. The century featured two church building booms after each of the World Wars, one related to the growth of suburban housing estates in the interwar period and the other to the reconstruction of wartime losses after the Second World War. There was considerable argument within the architectural profession about the merits of modernism versus traditionalism in style. These arguments influenced ecclesiastical architects, perhaps a little less than secular architects in the first half of the century, but that is not to say that they were without impact. After the Second World War the shortage of materials and urgent need to reconstruct led to the use of materials not widely used before in church construction, such as reinforced concrete. This in turn allowed for more flexible design strategies and the ability to experiment with new shapes. The interiors of churches, and their furnishings, were affected by these developments and by changes in the liturgy throughout the century, and it was these changes that had an impact on the installation of chancel screens. It is therefore not surprising that the majority of screens installed in the twentieth century were into existing churches. Screens were, however, still being introduced in new build projects in this period at least until the Second World War.

In the absence of any agreed paradigm for church building in the first half of the century, and the keen desire to avoid any of what were considered the old-fashioned ideas of the Ecclesiologists, texts such as Percy Dearmer's *Parson's Handbook*, the publications of the Alcuin Club and regulations of grant giving bodies such as the Incorporated Church Building Society were the most likely to be consulted when undertaking church work. Indeed, in the Twelfth Edition of the *Parson's Handbook* published in 1932 the inclusion of a chancel screen is assumed. Dearmer opines:

I do not think there is any difference of opinion among artists as to the great value of a well-designed rood-screen. It should not of course be solid except in cathedral and collegiate churches, but, solid or open, it gives the most splendid opportunity to the sculptor and painter. The screen should be of stone or wood and not a mere iron grating; but at the time it must not block out the high altar, nor hide the occupants of the stalls in a parish church.'[1]

Dearmer's view was one that was endorsed by the leading ecclesiastical architects of the first part of the century, many of whom had been articled to influential Victorian architects such as Bodley. Sir Charles Nicholson designed in excess of twenty screens and rood beams, and well-known establishment figures such as W. D. Caröe, Walter Tapper and Randoll Blacking also introduced screens into existing churches. There is a feeling of continuity with the previous centuries in their work.

At St Luke's Church, Rochdale (Lancashire) Frank Freeman finished the church designed by his father Knill Freeman in 1893, with the installation of a screen in 1914. So close is the resemblance of his work to a late Victorian design for this church by his father, that there is some debate as to whether this was Frank Freeman's design at all. The originally designed screen had not been put into the church at the time of construction due to lack of funds (not an uncommon problem). The description in *The Building News* is indicative of the attitude to this type of screen at the time:

The screen is so designed as to cause as little as possible obstruction of the view of the chancel and choir, the larger portion of the enrichment, cuspings, etc., being well above the eye level…The work is in the Decorated style of Gothic architecture, in harmony and keeping with the existing screens, and adds to the effect of an already dignified church.[2]

This screen also illustrates one of the problems with researching twentieth-century screens – their disappearance. Sadly, this church was demolished in 1979 and it is unclear what became of the screen, but there is little doubt that it would have been destroyed.

The inter-war years
After the First World War changes began in attitudes to church design both in existing and new churches. One of the most important developments that was to affect the existing church buildings was the

passing of the 1919 Assembly Powers Act, subsequently known as the Enabling Act. This Act formally created the Diocesan Advisory Committees (DACs) and focussed attention on the scrutiny of new work being introduced into old churches, the quality of design, and an increasing concern for conservation. Gothic design was seriously frowned upon, Victorian interiors were roundly condemned and re-orderings that whitewashed walls and simplified interiors were very much in vogue. Screens were carefully considered by the DACs both as new additions and when the conservation of existing examples was contemplated. The Central Council for the Care of Churches, the umbrella body for the DACs counselled vigilance over the loss of 'ancient woodwork' citing cases of a fourteenth century screen being

Fig. 1: St John the Baptist, Southend. Set up as a war memorial, it is unusual in depicting a soldier looking up to the crucified Christ. (Photo: Clare Price)

removed and burnt in a churchyard in 1917 and another case where screen panels had been made into an altar, remarking particularly that such woodwork should be 'scheduled for protection.'[3]

War memorials were a major concern in the early years of the DACs. Indeed, the precursors to the formal DAC system were committees started during the First World War after concern that the introduction of unregulated war memorials in churches was leading to the 'disfigurement' of the interiors of churches. They particularly discouraged the excessive quantities of memorial tablets being proposed to be fixed to the walls and favoured the dedication of fittings such as chancel screens instead. Indeed, many of the screens installed in existing churches in the years following the First World War were specifically war memorials and by far the greatest majority of screens installed across the whole period were memorials erected with the proceeds from a bequest. They generally conform to the design of Victorian chancel screens, perhaps due to intervention by DACs, rarely including any scenes of battle. One of a set of two screens and a Rood installed at St John the Baptist, Southend (Essex; Fig. 1) is unusual in this respect. Designed by Sir Charles Nicholson and carved by Harry Hems, it depicts a soldier on the battlefield looking with hope on the figure of Christ. If the intention was to create drama, it certainly succeeds.

The screen in Holy Trinity, Minchinhampton (Gloucestershire; Fig. 2) is more typical of those installed as war memorials. It was designed by one of the most accomplished designers of church interiors of the interwar period, F. C. Eden. Eden has been somewhat overlooked by historians as only two of his new church designs were built, despite having been highly influential and greatly respected during his lifetime. Having trained in the offices of Butterfield and Bodley, he spent his entire career as a sole practitioner. He worked closely with his close friends Sir Ninian Comper, Sir Charles Nicholson and Sir Walter Tapper, who were his contemporaries. He was prolific: Edward Hagger comments that his output included 'numerous chancels, chapels, screens, altars and...embroideries and furnishings of all kinds.'[4] The chancel screen was however his idea of the epitome of the correct English church furniture. Hagger states that 'Eden was unparalleled in his knowledge of extant examples of ancient screens' and was 'as proprietorial towards the English screen as Comper was to the idea of the English altar.'[5] Eden was also acutely aware of the relevance of context and the need to respect historic fabric after travels in France brought home to him the damage that could be done by extreme 'restorations'. Eden's reputation for fine work explains his popularity in the early twentieth century: as

Fig. 2: F. C. Eden's chancel screen at Holy Trinity, Minchinhampton. The screen is an essay in the study of medieval precedent.
(Photo: Clare Price)

Hagger comments, he 'had the enviable reputation of never putting a foot wrong'.[6] The screen at Minchinhampton is designed and executed to a very high standard, as was all his work. The screen and Rood are particularly significant within Eden's oeuvre as one of the very few that were unpainted. As can be seen from the later chancel ceiling decoration in the church, Eden favoured the use of colour in his projects. The fact

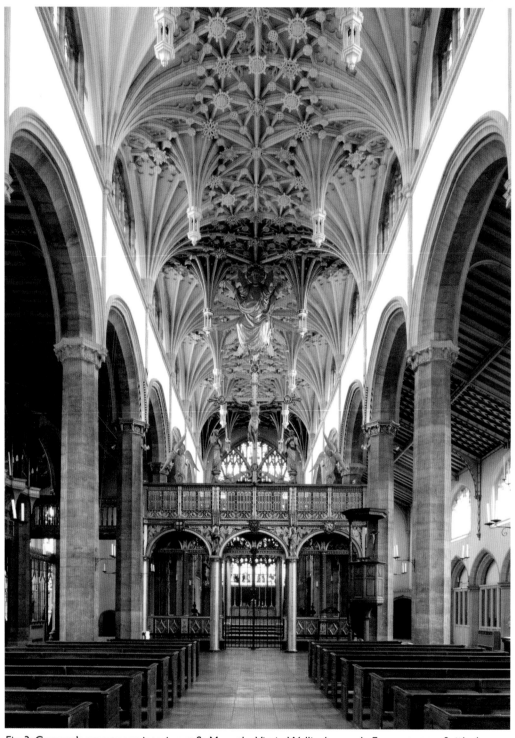

Fig. 3: Comper's sumptuous interior at St Mary the Virgin, Wellingborough. From start to finish the screen took 25 years to complete. (Photo: courtesy of Elain Harwood)

that this screen remains uncoloured, apparently at the request of the congregation, itself makes it very unusual. This screen is no longer in its original location but has been retained in the church being repurposed as a parclose screen with minor alterations to its size.

Eden was great friends with Sir Ninian Comper – someone who cannot be left out of any survey of twentieth-century church architects. Most of Comper's screenwork after the First World War dates from the 1920s after which the change in his philosophy of church design sees him move away from a medieval idiom to his 'Unity by Inclusion' phase, where he develops a new style based on a carefully researched use of a variety of elements from different periods. The church of St Mary the Virgin, Wellingborough (Northamptonshire; Fig. 3) has been seen as the culmination of all his ideas, as here he was able to use all the elements of 'Unity by Inclusion'. The church took over 26 years to complete. The chancel screen was begun in 1925, installation was finished in 1931 but the decoration of it continued until 1950. This chancel screen epitomises his approach, as he uses Classical arches but adds detail of both Italianate and Spanish influence. Describing it, Comper himself said:

> A high chancel screen has mouldings and acanthus straight from Classic Greece and a general design which is as much Italian as English, or English as Italian. The dragons on the rood loft are borrowed from medieval Greece, while the ironwork owes most to Spain.'[7]

Comper was deliberately an anti-establishment figure and ploughed his own furrow when it came to developing his ideas of the correct approach to church design. His work was unparalleled in its beauty and originality, but he was dismissed by many later commentators such as Niklaus Pevsner who considered a complete break from the past to be a necessity in new design. J. M. Richards summed up Comper's work as 'the last flowering of the Gothic Revival.'[8]

Sir Charles Nicholson embodied the antithesis of Comper's approach, in that he was a committed establishment figure. He was a prolific designer – who should be more widely appreciated – and unlike many of his contemporaries also wrote about his views throughout the period. In his 1914 church of St Alban, Copnor (Hampshire), Nicholson employs a Jacobean theme for the interior furnishing and includes an elaborate wooden painted chancel screen (Fig. 4). He was very clear on the importance of the inclusion of screens – in the preface to the 1911 book *Recent English Ecclesiastical Architecture* he states:

Fig. 4: Charles Nicholson's neo-Jacobean chancel screen at St Alban's, Copnor. Dykes Bower relocated this to the west end and, since, 2019, it now stands behind the font. The church has an active children's ministry. See also Fig. 7. (Photo: Clare Price)

A certain sense of restraint and seclusion is undoubtedly appropriate to the place in which the Holy Mysteries are celebrated. For this reason we do well in England to have preserved without a break up to the present day the ancient custom of veiling our chancels with screenwork. A chancel arch, such as it was customary to build in the days of 'Gothic with Bath stone trimmings' does not form a sufficient screening for the chancel, nor is it a feature of practical or artistic utility. Therefore it is best to dispense with a chancel arch and to spend the money on a proper rood-screen.[9]

These were views that he maintained throughout his long career.

During the 1930s, screens were introduced as part of larger re-furnishing projects. The annual reports of the DACs indicate a constant trickle of screens into existing churches, designed by the leading architects of the day. One such architect was Bernard Miller of Liverpool. His designs of modern churches, such as St Christopher's church, Withington in Manchester and St Christopher, Norris Green in Liverpool, are highly regarded and gained much press coverage on completion. His interest in modern design extended into art, and the screen he designed for Holy Cross, Woodchurch on the Wirral peninsula (executed by the artist Alan Durst) is potentially unique in its application of modern figurative motifs (Fig. 5).

Martin Travers is often associated with Anglo-Catholic decorative schemes, despite the wide variety of work that he undertook.[10] He completed the church of St John the Baptist, Harrow (London) in 1938–9 by adding a chapel and chancel with a screen to the original 1903 church by W. S. Alder, which had not been finished at the time due

Fig. 5: Holy Cross Woodchurch (Photo: courtesy of Holy Cross, Woodchurch)

to lack of funds.[11] The original designs for completing the church were too costly, and the DAC for London Diocese was forced to intervene to find another architect to complete the church. Their report for 1940 after Travers' work was completed, comments that 'the money saving has been considerable and has allowed the addition of some very fine fittings, an interesting screen to the chancel and chapel, a painted tympanum over the chancel arch, with good stalls and dignified altars.'[12] The project was considered to be an example of a 'successful addition of a chancel in contrasting style yet in a harmonious manner, with modern screen.'[13] Screens of a more modern, sparer design, of which Harrow is an example, were more typical of those that were being designed for new churches towards the end of the interwar period. For new churches it is clear that any form of gothic was considered to be unfashionable and as a result new screens in these contexts became increasingly minimal in design. Indeed, in some cases the imperative that the altar should be clearly visible reduced screens to a mere framework.

The new church of John Keble, Mill Hill in the London Diocese, was designed in 1933 to commemorate the centenary of the preaching of the Assize Sermon by John Keble (generally considered to be the date that marks the beginning of the Oxford Movement): hence its unique dedication. This association prompted the involvement of a number of very significant personalities in the ecclesiastical world at the time. It was lauded by the architectural press for its modern design as soon as it was completed and later was to take on even more significance, being considered ahead of its time in its liturgical arrangement. The church was designed after a competition – this in itself was unusual for churches. The parish wrote their own competition brief and chose five architects

Figs. 6a (*this page*) and 6b (*opposite*): John Keble Church, Mill Hill. Donald Martin-Smith's designs for the interior, first without a screen, revised to include one at the request of the parish, though it was decided not to proceed. (Photos: courtesy of John Keble Church, Mill Hill)

to compete: N. F. Cachemaille-Day, J. Harold Gibbons, Professor A. B. Knapp-Fisher, Frederick Etchells and Donald Martin-Smith. Martin-Smith was an unknown in church design who happened to be the brother of the Director of Music at Mill Hill. The choice of architects does not indicate that the congregation were necessarily looking for a modern building (with the exception of Cachemaille-Day). Knapp-Fisher, Gibbons and Etchells were not known for their modern designs and their competition entries were for remarkably traditional longitudinal churches. The two crucial requirements in the competition brief were that the choir should be in the midst of the congregation, and that the guidelines of the Alcuin Club should be followed. The Alcuin Club's publications followed the traditional stance of Percy Dearmer. Donald Martin-Smith won the competition after the adjudicator, Edward Maufe judged that his design alone fulfilled the choir location requirements. The choir was placed in the centre of the nave and complied with the Alcuin Club requirements, complete with returned stalls for the clergy. The Alcuin Club also recommended a chancel screen. The Building Committee of the Parish requested that, instead of the hanging cross that Martin-Smith had drawn on his original perspectives (Fig. 6a), it be replaced by a 'light screen…that might well carry a small cross over the central arch'.[14] As a result, Martin-Smith revised his design, adding a screen complete with crucifix and attendant Rood figures (Fig. 6b). Members of the committee expressed concern over the design and it was agreed that W. H. Randoll Blacking, an ecclesiastical architect and expert on fittings, be consulted.[15] The outcome of this consultation, after considerable discussion was that: 'the sub-committee decided that after careful consideration the architectural grounds for omitting

the choir screen and Rood clearly outweighed the liturgical grounds for its inclusion.'[16] It is significant that it is the architectural grounds that won the day in this design. Clearly the screen did not work with the architecture of the building, but it shows that the parish were attempting to follow the liturgical guidelines, despite the modernity of the architecture.

This church also illustrates the difficulty being faced by many parishes building new churches at this time. The requirements of bodies that would give them grants to build assumed a traditional longitudinal church with a chancel and nave preferably separated by a screen. Increasingly the economic situation required cheaper ways of building to be explored and simplicity of design to be championed. Often these buildings just were not architecturally suitable for a screen. Even when the buildings were longitudinal and the parish would have liked a screen, often financial strictures meant that they could not afford much in the way of fittings at the outset. Screens were a casualty of this situation.

The reassessment of screens in the late-twentieth century

The outbreak of the Second World War coincided with considerable renewed controversy about the use of chancel screens. An increasing groundswell of opinion, based on a perception of Early Church practice wholly different to that of previous generations (as discussed in earlier chapters in this volume), emphasised that church buildings should allow the congregation to see and hear everything that happened at the altar and that choirs should not obstruct this but be removed to the rear of the church. The chancel screen was more often than not considered an obstruction to this visual openness. But those favouring the traditional arrangements were not easily persuaded. A long running dispute in *The Times* in 1939–40 revolving around the location of a screen culminated in a furious letter from the Revd Andrew Freeman of Standish who disagreed with this new direction in church design. He said, 'It is clear that there are quite a large number of people who will not rest content till they can see from end to end in every great church.' He urged that 'something must be done' to curb the 'advocates of the vista' and that 'those who object to the vista on aesthetic and liturgical grounds must not stand idle until the next assault begins.'[17]

The destruction of many churches in the Second World War was to increase the urgency for building cheaper and more basic churches as fast as possible. In contrast to the interwar period where a dearth of written material giving guidance on the building of a new church had given Dearmer such a hold over design, immediately after the

Second World War there was a flurry of publishing of both books and articles. The end of the war had brought the need for a concerted effort on church building into sharp focus, and attempts were therefore made to provide guidance on the building of new churches and the repair of those existing churches that had suffered bomb damage. The majority of these post-war publications do not mention screens at all. Of those that do, in Short's edited volume of 1947 *Post War Church Building* the only mention is in an essay on furnishing a church by Llewellyn Williams, which very tellingly only refers to examples of screens from the previous century, except for a mention of those at Edward Maufe's 1932 church of St Thomas the Apostle, Hanwell, in London.[18] These are very beautiful but are in fact parclose screens - this church does not have a chancel screen.

In contrast, G. W. O. Addleshaw and Frederick Etchells in their book *The Architectural Setting of Anglican Worship* (also published in 1947) trace the use of screens throughout the history of the Anglican church as part of their examination of historic architectural developments before tackling the current issues. They conclude their survey with a chapter entitled 'The Present Opportunity' in which they comment that:

> The destruction caused by the war and the consequent cessation of church building, taken together with modern methods of construction available present an extraordinary opportunity not likely to happen again…to adapt the principles of the classical Anglican tradition to the present day problems…whether in connection with the rebuilding of destroyed churches or the re-adaptation of medieval or later buildings to modern needs, or the construction of entirely new churches.[19]

Addleshaw and Etchells were keen to promote a type of church suitable for the Prayer Book and favoured a sixteenth century auditory church form. They were highly critical of the use of screens during the Victorian period and commented that the screen had been 'allowed to separate the clergy and the choir in the chancel from the people in the nave.' They were not totally against screens though, going on to say that 'though it is a departure from the best in our tradition to permit a screen to divide the priest from his people in public worship, this does not involve the banishing of screens from our churches.'[20]

Interestingly, Addleshaw and Etchells advocated the use of a nave altar as the principal altar for the main services, turning the chancel of traditional longitudinal churches into a chapel for smaller services by inserting a chancel screen. They conclude that:

The chancel screen would thus, instead of dividing the people from the clergy and the altar, serve a purpose, very legitimate in Anglican ecclesiology, of separating the church into two main parts one for… lesser services…and one for all the main services.[21]

This approach became very influential in re-ordering projects in the second half of the century, especially as the influence of the Liturgical Movement began to affect the layout of churches. An early example can be seen in the re-ordering of Cuddesdon church (Oxfordshire). Stephen Dykes Bower was commissioned to carry out an ambitious reordering in 1939, providing screens all around the crossing, which was never completed, being curtailed by the start of the War. The 1941 screen turned the chancel in to a chapel via the insertion of a screen that also acted as a reredos for a new nave altar. This screen is of the 'reja' or Spanish type of wrought iron, classical in style and painted gold and black[22] (Percy Dearmer would have thoroughly disapproved). Stephen Dykes Bower was an architect of great sensitivity in church design. Like his long-term friend and mentor F. C. Eden, he was an admirer of the then unfashionable Victorian architects such as Pearson and Bodley. He is best known for his work extending the parish church at Bury St Edmunds to transform it into a cathedral – work that finished as recently as 2005. He was unique in the post-war period for continuing to design in the gothic tradition, and valued craftsmanship, good detail and fine colouring. His use of colour can be seen particularly well in his post-war work at St Alban's, Copnor (Hampshire). I believe this church to be unique in having two twentieth-century chancel screens. The original Nicholson church was bombed in 1941, resulting in the complete destruction of the west end. Stephen Dykes Bower was commissioned to rebuild it, a long job that lasted from 1956 to 1972. A nave altar was also required here, and Dykes Bower again inserted a new Renaissance style chancel screen turning the chancel into a chapel (Fig. 7).[23] He re-coloured and relocated Nicholson's chancel screen to the west end to create a narthex which functioned as a baptistery. Re-ordering at this church has led to the very recent (2019) relocation of Nicholson's screen once again: this time to behind the font.

These developments lead to the question: when does a chancel screen become a reredos or parclose screen? To answer this, it is necessary to consider all the functions of such a screen. For example, in another Dykes Bower project – St Paul's, Salford (Greater Manchester) – a light wrought-iron chancel screen was again inserted as a backdrop to the nave altar, but in this case the high altar was retained and used.[24]

Fig. 7: Dykes Bower's chancel screen at St Alban's, Copnor, which replaced Nicholson's earlier screen. See also Fig. 4. (Photo: Clare Price)

This perhaps justifies the continued classification of such screens as chancel screens.

In the 1950s a few new churches were fitted with chancel screens. Some of those with screens had been designed before the war and building works had been delayed due to the restriction on building materials. Caröe and Partners designed a traditional brick church in New Addington (Surrey) in 1958 and included a simple screen with attached pulpit and lectern, which was relocated following reordering to behind the nave altar. However, the increasing emphasis on Holy

Communion as a corporate act and the consequent need for the altar to be brought down into the midst of the people, as strongly advocated by Peter Hammond in his polemic *Liturgy and Architecture* of 1960,[25] left no place for the chancel screen. Major ecclesiastical architects of the post-war period such as George Pace advocated a complete *tabula rasa* for the design of church interiors, developing new furnishings that avoided historicist references. Pace himself was also deeply concerned that what he called the 'historical conscience' would prevent the fitting of existing churches with new furnishing schemes and excessive claims for conservation.[26] He appreciated the interiors created by the likes of Eden, Comper and Travers as being 'theological affirmations' which were 'pearls beyond price' but also recognised that many considered them of no relevance in the post-war world.[27]

However, against this backdrop it is possible to identify a residual effect of the chancel screen – a last vestige perhaps. Despite the openness of the churches there remains a need to highlight and delineate the most sacred part of the church from the congregation. One of the features of the modern spare screens of the interwar period was the lack of Rood figures. The image of the suffering Christ on the cross is rarely seen in these modern style churches, but a plain cross without a figure is sometimes substituted. The post-war period sees a return of representations of Christ on a cross in the form of hanging Roods – but there is an important change which correlates with a move away from the medieval ideas to those of the early church. The Anglican advocate of the Liturgical Movement, Gabriel Hebert, promoting the return to Early Church participatory worship described the shift to the emphasis on individual devotions of the congregation during the Middle Ages in this way:

> In early times the church was dominated by the figure of the glorified Christ in the apse above the altar: now the crucifix becomes common. The earliest crucifixes show Him robed and crowned, the Victor reigning from the tree: but gradually the crucifixion descends from heaven to earth, till finally the eyes of Christ are closed in death, and we see a realistic view of human suffering…all this illustrates the change which had taken place from the 'ontological' idea of the mystery and of the sacramental fellowship of the Body, to a new emphasis on the psychological experience of the individual.[28]

This motif of the glorified Christ – taken from this *retour au sources* – represents the desire to return to the Early Church unsullied by the later divisions and vicissitudes that plagued the church: a revival of the 'maiestas' can be identified as a result. It becomes popular not just behind the altar, but is sometimes employed as a hanging motif on the notional line between the chancel and the nave, forming a signal as a screen also does, that the space beyond it has heightened significance within the building. An example can be seen in the 1962 church of St Edmund, Northwood Hills (London) by Cachemaille-Day (Fig. 8).

St Paul's Church at Bow Common in London was perhaps the most revolutionary church of the early post-war period in the Anglican church due to the philosophy behind its design (Fig. 9). Writing about St Paul's in *Churchbuilding* magazine, Robert Maguire and Keith Murray emphasised how the architecture was intended to focus on the importance of the altar as a place of sacrifice and a place of a communal meal – calling these 'complementary concepts.'[29] The concept of sacrifice however seems to get lost as they describe all the features of the church in terms of communality. They contended that 'too many steps [up to the altar] (characteristic of most Gothic Revival churches and continued in many modern churches) speaks only of sacrifice' and 'tends to cut off' the altar and the priest from the congregation; the corona defines the sanctuary but again avoids the problem of traditional layouts which

Fig. 8: The hanging rood at Cachemaille-Day's 1962 St Edmund's, Northwood Hills. (Photo: Clare Price)

Fig. 9: St Paul's, Bow Common, by Robert Maguire and Keith Murray. (Photo: courtesy of Elain Harwood)

they accused of cutting off 'the sanctuary from the rest of the church tending to make the Eucharist appear as something *performed* in the sanctuary and *observed* by those outside' (italics in the original).[30] Here, therefore, the corona almost takes the role of the screen by delineating the extent of the most significant part of the church – 'it defines the space of the sanctuary without being a barrier.'[31] It is striking however, that the view when walking through the main ceremonial doors momentarily gives the impression that there is a suspended metal chancel screen. This resolves into the corona when you appreciate that it surrounds the sanctuary.

Conclusion

In conclusion, it can be seen that trends in twentieth-century church design created a perfect storm for chancel screens. The early part of the century was dominated by a tradition emanating from the Victorians that persisted despite the increasing rejection of the gothic and the plan form that typified it. Many very fine screens were designed and installed in this period. The screen endured in modern designs, its liturgical importance acknowledged, and the design simplified. In existing churches, the chancel screen became a key asset in reordering, serving the dual function of reredos and screen. With the emphasis on corporate worship, the Liturgical Reform Movement – which advocated a central altar around which the congregation could gather for a fully participatory act of worship – changed the shape of churches, and the location for a screen was lost. But the need to form some delineation around the sanctuary remained and residual features such as the hanging Rood and corona speak of the continuing need for the screen's function. As the century progressed it is clear that, due to the changing philosophy in both the performance of the liturgy and ecclesiastical architectural design, the introduction of new chancel screens waned – their design becoming increasingly spare and minimal – eventually disappearing altogether. What began the century valued as 'a considerable devotional and artistic asset',[32] by the close was perceived as an 'obstruction to worshippers.'[33]

Notes

1. Percy Dearmer, *Parson's Handbook,* (12th Edition), (1932), 51.
2. Anon., 'New Oak Chancel Screen St, Luke's Church, Rochdale', *The Building News* 3099, (29 May 1914), 735.
3. Central Council for the Care of Churches, *The Protection of Our English Churches Seventh Report for 1934–7,* (1937), 43.
4. Edward Hagger, 'F. C. Eden: Building on Tradition' in *Twentieth Century Architecture,* vol. 3 (1998), 75–84 (p. 77).
5. Hagger, *Twentieth Century Architecture,* 79.
6. Hagger, *Twentieth Century Architecture,* 80.
7. Anthony Symondson and Stephen Arthur Bucknall, *Sir Ninian Comper, An Introduction to his Life and Work,* (Reading, 2006), 190.
8. Symondson and Bucknall, *Sir Ninian Comper,* 197.
9. C. A. Nicholson, 'The Design and Arrangement of Churches' in Mervyn Macartney (ed.) *Recent English Ecclesiastical Architecture,* (1911), 6–12 (p. 9).
10. Michael Yelton, *Martin Travers, His Life and Work,* (Salisbury, 2016), 114.
11. Central Council for the Care of Churches, *The Care of Churches their upkeep and protection, Eighth Report,* (1940), 33.
12. CCCC, *The Care of Churches,* (1940), 34.
13. CCCC, *The Care of Churches,* (1940), 35.
14. John Keble Mill Hill Building Committee meeting minutes 4 May 1935, uncatalogued London Diocesan Fund file, London Metropolitan Archives.
15. John Keble Mill Hill Building Committee meeting minutes 27 January 1936, uncatalogued London Diocesan Fund file, London Metropolitan Archives.

16. John Keble Mill Hill Building Sub-Committee for Liturgical Furnishing meeting minutes 11 June 1936, uncatalogued London Diocesan Fund file, London Metropolitan Archives.

17. Andrew Freeman, 'Letters' *The Times*, (12 Feb 1940), 4.

18. Llewellyn E. Williams, 'Church Woodwork: Pews, Pulpits, Altar Rails and Screens.' In Ernest Short (ed.), *Post War Church Building* (1947), 173–184, (p. 181).

19. G. W. O. Addleshaw and Frederick Etchells, *The Architectural Setting of Anglican Worship*, (1947), 225.

20. Addleshaw and Etchells, *Architectural Setting*, 238.

21. Addleshaw and Etchells, *Architectural Setting*, 241.

22. Anthony Symondson, *Stephen Dykes Bower*, (2011), 18.

23. Symondson, *Dykes Bower*, 120–21.

24. Ken Powell 'Enrichment as revival: re-using church fittings', *Country Life*, (17 April 1986), 1026–1028 (p. 1026).

25. Peter Hammond, *Liturgy and Architecture*, (1960), 35.

26. George G. Pace, 'Principles and Precepts' in G. Cope (ed.) *Making the Building Serve the Liturgy* (1962), 53–56 (pp. 54–55).

27. George G. Pace, 'Architecture and Architect in the Service of the Church' in W. Lockett (ed.) *The Modern Architectural Setting of the Liturgy*, (1964), 78–92 (p. 89).

28. Gabriel Hebert, *Liturgy and Society: the Function of the Church in the Modern World*, (1935), 83.

29. R. Maguire and K. Murray, 'Anglican Church in Stepney, *Churchbuilding*, 7 (October 1962), 14–22 (p. 16).

30. Maguire and Murray 'Anglican Church' 16.

31. Maguire and Murray 'Anglican Church' 22.

32. W. H. Randoll Blacking, *The Arrangement and Furnishing of a Church*, (*c.*1950 - not dated), 6.

33. *Pace* Randoll Blacking whose words I have misquoted here wilfully. The full quote reads 'A well designed screen…can be a considerable devotional and artistic asset; the screens to be seen in some of the post-Reformation churches as well as in some modern ones clearly show that they need cause no obstruction to worshippers.'

The Ecclesiological Society

The Ecclesiological Society is for all those who love churches and are interested in their fabric and furnishings, their use and conservation. The society was founded in 1879, as a successor to the Cambridge Camden Society of 1839. It has a lively programme including lectures, visits and an annual conference. Members also receive the society's publications – *Ecclesiology Today*, *Church Crawler* and the proceedings of our annual conference – as well as regular e-mail newsletters.

Membership is open to all. For further details, see the society's website, www.ecclsoc.org, or write to the Hon. Membership Secretary at the email address given overleaf.

Charity registration

The Society is a registered charity, number 210501. Its registered address, which should not be used for general correspondence, is c/o The Society of Antiquaries of London, Burlington House, Piccadilly, London W1V 0HS.

Membership subscriptions

Life member (UK only)	£300.00
Annual member (UK)	£17.50
Under 25/retired (UK)	£14.00
Extra household member at same address	£3.50
Overseas membership: please enquire.	

Contributions to *Ecclesiology Today*

The Editor is always pleased to receive articles for consideration, or suggestions for proposed contributions, either fully worked out or, preferably, at an early stage in development.

In furtherance of the society's aims, articles should promote 'the study of the arts, architecture and liturgy of the Christian Church'. Articles will generally be based on fresh research, investigation or analysis, or have some topical relevance to the design, conservation or study of church buildings. Most articles are objective and factual but there is the opportunity for well-argued personal views on matters of wide interest to be put forward in our occasional 'Viewpoint' series.

Articles which deal with an individual building are welcome, provided they go beyond a general account of the church to either highlight matters of wider significance or explore a particular aspect of the building in depth.

There is no formal process of peer-review, but articles will usually be sent to one or more readers with relevant knowledge or experience of the subject matter for an independent opinion. Publication may depend on making changes in response to their recommendations.

Contributions should be prepared in accordance with the guidelines for contributors which can be found on our website, or obtained from the Editor.

Books for review should be sent to the Reviews Editor (contact details opposite).